Editorial Project Manager
Erica N. Russikoff, M.A.

Editor in Chief
Karen J. Goldfluss, M.S. Ed.

Creative Director
Sarah M. Fournier

Illustrator
Mark Mason

Art Coordinator
Renée Mc Elwee

Cover Artist
Diem Pascarella

Imaging
Amanda R. Harter

Publisher
Mary D. Smith, M.S. Ed.

Author

Tracie Heskett, M. Ed.

For correlations to the Common Core State Standards, see pages 107–112 of this book or visit *http://www.teachercreated.com/standards/*.

Teacher Created Resources
12621 Western Avenue
Garden Grove, CA 92841
www.teachercreated.com
ISBN: 978-1-4206-8389-9

© 2016 Teacher Created Resources
Made in U.S.A.

Table of Contents

Introduction

Approaching Math Content— Today's Standards

The Common Core State Standards address several important goals in education:

- to prepare students for college and careers
- to develop critical-thinking and analytical skills students need for success
- to help teachers measure student progress and achievement throughout the year

The Common Core Mathematics Standards seek to provide teachers and students with focused mathematics instruction. The standards are designed to deepen students' understanding as they progress through grade levels and topics.

Mathematics is a subject in which concepts build in a progression. A strong foundation of basic concepts must be laid, beginning in the early grades. The Common Core State Standards recognize this learning sequence. Mathematical thinking is divided into several broad categories, referred to as "domains." Elementary grades address the same general domains, with specific standards for student understanding and achievement within each domain. For grades 1–5, these domains include Operations & Algebraic Thinking, Number & Operations in Base Ten, Number & Operations—Fractions (begins in grade 3), Measurement & Data, and Geometry.

It is important for students to understand the role mathematics plays in everyday life. The Common Core Mathematics Standards encourage students to apply their mathematical knowledge to real-world problems and situations. Teachers, in turn, assess student understanding and mastery of concepts by asking them to explain their thinking and justify their answers. Word problems provide students with opportunities for the practical application of mathematical concepts.

> This book presents word problems in a realistic setting. Students dig into the content of each "scenario" as they apply math concepts to solve multiple problems. Each unit is designed to encourage students to read for understanding, revisit content on a variety of levels, and use information as a tool for solving more complex problems.

Establishing Mathematical Practices

The Common Core Standards for Mathematical Practice (SMP) describe practices students can implement to help them engage with mathematical content. As your students work through the activities in this book, encourage them to develop these habits as they practice and develop problem-solving skills.

1. Make sense of problems and persevere in solving them.
2. Reason abstractly and quantitatively.
3. Construct viable arguments and critique the reasoning of others.
4. Model with mathematics.
5. Use appropriate tools strategically.
6. Attend to precision.
7. Look for and make use of structure.
8. Look for and express regularity in repeated reasoning.

These practices help students understand core mathematical concepts so they can apply a variety of strategies for successful problem solving. As students learn underlying principles, they will be able to . . .

- consider similar problems.
- represent problems in ways that make sense.
- justify conclusions and explain their reasoning.
- apply mathematics to practical situations.
- use technology to work with mathematics.
- explain concepts to other students.
- consider a broad overview of a problem.
- deviate from a known procedure to use an appropriate shortcut.
- reason and explain why a mathematical statement is true.
- explain and apply appropriate mathematical rules.

Help your students and their families find success. Work with administrators, other teachers, and parents to plan and hold math-coaching nights for parents. The tips on page 6 may be helpful for parents as they work with students at home. Consider photocopying the page to send home in students' homework folders to aid with math assignments. Additionally, prepare a visual aid to help parents understand students' work in math. Share this aid with parents at back-to-school night or on other occasions when they visit the classroom.

How to Use This Book

This book contains several mathematical problem-solving units. Each unit gives students the opportunity to practice and develop one or more essential mathematical skills. Units are grouped by domains—although within a unit, more than one domain may be addressed. Within each domain, math concepts build on one another, forming a foundation for student learning and understanding. In addition to the Common Core Mathematics Standards covered in this book, the passages that accompany each unit meet one or more English Language Arts Standards as they provide practice reading appropriate literature and nonfiction text.

About the Units

Each unit is three pages in length. Depending on the needs of your students, you may wish to introduce units in small-group or whole-class settings using a guided-to-independent approach. Reading the passages and responding to activities in collaborative groups allows students to share and support their problem-solving results.

As an alternative, students can work independently and compare responses with others. Whichever method you choose, the reading and math activities will provide students with the tools they need to build mathematical knowledge for today's more rigorous math standards.

All units begin with a reading passage that presents a mathematical problem or situation. Engaging nonfiction and fiction passages are included in the book. Passages are age-level appropriate and fall within a range of 740 to 940 on the Lexile scale.

Each passage incorporates information to be used for solving practical math problems. They also allow students to experience a variety of genres and make meaningful connections between math and reading.

Students practice reading skills as they read for understanding, revisit text on a variety of levels, and use passage information as a tool for solving more complex problems.

Sidebars provide tips to help students think about how to do the math. In addition, they offer tools or strategies students can use throughout the problem–solving process.

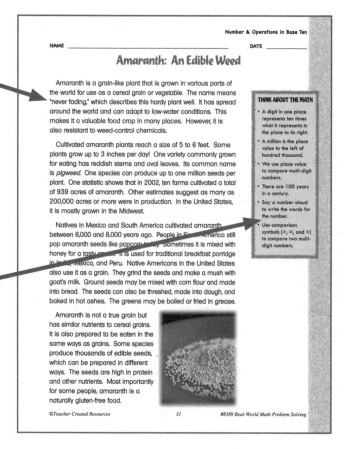

About the Units (cont.)

Page 2

The second page of each unit introduces problem-solving tasks. Space is provided for students to draw pictures, work out their answers, write equations, show their work, and explain their thinking. Students are asked to use the unit passage to respond to reading content and investigate the text in order to find solutions to the problems on the page.

The questions require students to look back at the text for clues and information that relates to each question. They must then interpret this information in a way that helps them solve each task on the page. In doing so, students learn to support their responses with concrete evidence.

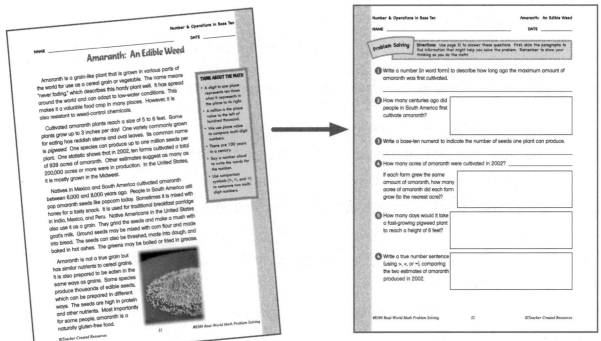

Page 3

The *Engage* option extends the mathematical situation with questions that allow students to look back at the reading passage and use critical-thinking skills.

The activities in this section strengthen students' comprehension skills by posing questions or situations for which further reflection of the text is required. Questions may be open-ended and require higher-level thinking skills and supported responses. Activities in this section focus on a combination of reading and math skills.

While students can respond independently to the activities on this page, you may wish to have them discuss their answers with a partner, in a small group, or with the entire class. This method can also provide closure to the unit.

The Path to Common Core Success: A Parent's Guide

Your child's success is measured by much more than numbers or grades. Being successful includes feeling confident and gaining practical skills to help students in life. The following tips will help you work with your child at home to understand the mathematics he or she is learning at school.

- Attend any curriculum or math-coaching nights offered by the school.

- Become familiar with the Standards for Mathematical Practice, which explain how students should apply math concepts and principles.

- Become familiar with the mathematical content standards, which explain what students should know about math and be able to do.

- Ask your child to explain the underlying concept of a math problem or the "main idea."

- Talk together about the core concept of a mathematical task to ensure your child understands it.

- Encourage your child to use concrete objects to model and demonstrate math problems.

- Talk with your child and help him or her to restate math problems in his or her own words.

- Have your child teach you one new strategy for solving a particular type of math problem.

- Discuss (parents and children) how a given strategy might be helpful to solve a particular problem.

- Discuss different ways a problem could be solved.

- Encourage your child to check that his or her solution is accurate and makes sense.

- Talk about ways math rules and concepts apply to specific problems.

- Explain how you used math that day at work or in your daily life.

- Help your child make connections between the day's homework and real life applications.

- Support your child in the process of learning to think critically and analytically.

- Practice patience together with your child as you work on math together.

- Support your child as he or she develops additional reading skills.

NAME _____   DATE _____

Wolves & Coyotes

Wolves

Weight: 60–120 lbs.   **Height:** 27–33 in.   **Length:** 5–6 ft.

Coloring: white, black, shades of brown and gray

- long legs, large feet
- large nose pad and broad snout
- howls, seldom barks

Territory range varies depending on factors such as available prey, terrain, climate, and the presence of other wolf packs.

A wolf pack territory may be less than 100 square miles in the United States. Farther north, in Canada, territories may be over 300 square miles or more.

Coyotes

Weight: 24–45 lbs.   **Height:** 20–22 in.   **Length:** $3\frac{1}{2}$–$4\frac{1}{2}$ ft.

Coloring: similar to wolves, often reddish hues, not all white or all black

- shorter legs, small feet
- long, pointed snout
- howls mixed with yips and barks

Territories depend on availability of prey. A coyote in a forest might require 60 square miles or more. In urban areas, the territory might be one-fifth that size.

THINK ABOUT THE MATH

- Use multiplication to compare amounts.
- The phrase "*x* times as many" can be rewritten as a multiplication equation.
- Compare amounts by saying one amount is *x* times as many as another amount.
- Sometimes an amount cannot be equally divided into groups. The amount left over is called a remainder.
- Remainders can be included in an answer to a problem, or they can be used to round the answer to a problem and then not be included in the answer.
- Use a letter to stand for an unknown number in a problem.
- Use estimation to check an answer.
- There are 12 inches in 1 foot.

NAME _____   DATE _____

Directions: Use page 7 to answer these questions. First, skim the paragraphs to find information that might help you solve the problem. Remember to show your thinking as you do the math!

1 Write an equation that could be used to find how many times larger a small wolf is by weight than a small coyote.

Now use rounding and estimation to solve the equation.

Write an equation that could be used to find how many times larger a large wolf is by weight than a large coyote.

Now use rounding and estimation to solve the equation.

2 Inches could be used to describe the lengths of these animals.

How many inches long is a wolf? _____

A coyote? _____

Write equations to show your thinking.

3 Feet could be used to describe the heights of these animals.

About how many feet tall is a wolf? _____

A coyote? _____

Write equations to show your thinking.

4 Write and solve an equation to show how many times larger wolf territories in Canada are than in the United States.

5 Coyotes in urban areas do not require as much territory because there is more prey. How much territory do they need compared to coyotes in forests?

What is the size of an urban territory in square miles? Write an equation.

NAME _____   DATE _____

1 Write 2–3 sentences to summarize the differences between wolves and coyotes.

_____

_____

_____

2 In what ways do the territories of wolves and coyotes differ? _____

_____

_____

3 What is one thing you learned from your research about differences or similarities in the behavior of wolves and coyotes?

_____

_____

4 What did you learn about the population status of these animals? Is either endangered? Why or why not?

_____

_____

_____

_____

5 What reasons might you have for learning more about wolves or coyotes? What difference could your learning make in your life or the lives of others?

_____

_____

_____

_____

NAME _____   DATE _____

My Shadow*

I have a little shadow that goes in and out with me,
And what can be the use of him is more than I can see.
He is very, very like me from the heels up to the head;
And I see him jump before me, when I jump into my bed.

The funniest thing about him is the way he likes to grow—
Not at all like proper children, which is always very slow;
For he sometimes shoots up taller like an India-rubber ball,
And he sometimes gets so little that there's none of him at all.

He hasn't got a notion of how children ought to play,
And can only make a fool of me in every sort of way.
He stays so close beside me, he's a coward you can see;
I'd think shame to stick to nursie as that shadow sticks to me!

One morning, very early, before the sun was up,
I rose and found the shining dew on every buttercup;
But my lazy little shadow, like an arrant sleepy-head,
Had stayed at home behind me and was fast asleep in bed.

THINK ABOUT THE MATH

- The phrase "*x* times as many" can be rewritten as a multiplication equation.

- Compare lengths by saying one length is *x* times as long as another length.

- There are 12 inches in 1 foot.

- Write a multiplication equation to compare amounts of things.

- Draw pictures to show what is happening in a comparison problem.

- Use a letter to stand for an unknown number in a problem.

- Use smaller units to express and define larger measurement units.

*by Robert Louis Stevenson, 1850–1894

Photograph by Ghislain Berger, CC BY 2.0.

NAME _____   DATE _____

Problem Solving   **Directions:** Think about shadows you have observed and use the relationships between multiplication and division, place-value strategies, and estimation and rounding to answer the questions below.

1 Mrs. Cotter's shadow is 127 inches in the morning. It is 33 inches at noon. About how many times longer is the shadow in the morning?

Her shadow is 62 inches in the late afternoon. About how many times longer is it in the late afternoon than at noon?

Later in the evening the shadow is 201 inches. What is the difference between the morning and evening shadows?

2 Mrs. Cotter is 5 feet 4 inches tall. How many inches tall is she?

At what time of day is her shadow closest to her actual height?

3 Use the back of this page to create a chart showing lengths of shadows.

If possible, measure your shadow and that of other people or objects. Make a chart to show the length of each shadow in the morning, at noon, and in the late afternoon. Use standard measurement units to compare the shadows.

Write one or more equations to compare the lengths of shadows.

Write a sentence to summarize your findings. _____

_____

_____

NAME _____ DATE _____

Engage **Directions:** Think about shadows as described in the poem. Then, answer the questions below.

1 What causes a shadow? _____

_____

_____

2 Why does a shadow "stick to" the poet? _____

_____

_____

3 What causes the growing and shrinking of the shadow mentioned in the second stanza?

_____

_____

_____

4 Why was the shadow not with the poet in the last stanza? _____

_____

_____

_____

5 What purpose can shadows serve? _____

_____

_____

_____

NAME _____   DATE _____

Matthew Henson: A Frozen Frontier

Matthew Henson was born in a family of freeborn sharecroppers a year after the end of the Civil War. During his teen years, he worked on a sailing ship, where he learned many technical skills. He also learned to read and write. After the captain of the ship died, Henson left his life at sea to work as a shop clerk.

One day, Robert Peary came to the shop with a load of pelts. Henson was still very interested in a life of travel and adventure. Peary was impressed with Matthew's experience and asked Matthew to join him on his next assignment. Together they mapped the jungle of Nicaragua in the hopes of finding a route for a canal between the Atlantic and Pacific Oceans. This journey established a firm friendship between the two men.

A few years later, Peary again invited Henson to join him on explorations and expeditions in the Arctic. Henson's expertise and skills contributed to the success of their journeys. Each expedition led them closer to the North Pole. In 1906, they came within 174 miles of the North Pole. Peary's observations showed they reached 87 degrees N latitude. Over the years, they covered over 9,000 miles on dogsleds across Greenland and Canada.

They began their final expedition for the Pole in 1908 and made the final push in the spring of 1909. Peary insisted Henson be part of the team, saying, "Henson must go all the way. I can't make it there without him." Supply teams followed them to the final camp. A final team consisting of Peary, Henson, and four Inuit natives took five dogsleds toward the Pole. In that five-day march, they traveled more than 170 miles, pushing 12 to 14 hours a day. Their hope was to make it there and back before huge cracks opened in the ice, blocking their way. On the fifth day, Peary took measurements of their location at noon and hoisted the flag at the geographic pole, right behind their igloos. Man had reached the North Pole!

THINK ABOUT THE MATH

- Sometimes an amount cannot be equally divided into groups. The amount left over is called a remainder.

- Sometimes a remainder can be discarded.

- Think about how accurate your final answer needs to be to determine if you can use estimation to solve a problem.

- Use a letter to stand for an unknown number in an equation.

- Use mental math to see if your answer makes sense.

NAME _____   DATE _____

Problem Solving | **Directions:** Use page 13 to answer these questions. First, skim the paragraphs to find information that might help you solve the problem. Remember to show your thinking as you do the math!

1 If the final push took 5 days and they traveled 170 miles, how many miles did the team travel per day?

How fast would they have had to travel to make it in 4 days?

2 If they traveled at least 12 hours per day, what was their speed in miles per hour? Use rounding to estimate their speed. (Use the information from question 1 for your calculations.)

If they traveled 14 hours per day at this speed, how many miles would they cover?

3 The North Pole is said to be located at 90 degrees N latitude. How many degrees did Peary and Henson come within the Pole in 1906?

4 Today, a temporary base camp is set up in the spring. Large tents rest on pack ice 3 feet thick, solid enough for ice planes to land. From there, explorers cross-country ski the remaining 5 miles to the Pole. That last leg of the journey takes about 3 hours.

Use estimation and rounding to find how far cross-country skiers travel in one hour as they ski to the North Pole.

NAME _____   DATE _____

| Engage | **Directions:** Research with classmates to learn more about the geographic North Pole. Use the following links to help you: |

- *http://education.nationalgeographic.com/encyclopedia/north-pole/*
- *http://www.ducksters.com/geography/north_pole.php*
- *http://water.usgs.gov/edu/gallery/watercyclekids/icecap-greenland.html*

1 How do we define the North Pole? _____

_____

2 What about this location helps people navigate and find their way? _____

_____

3 How does its location affect the amount of daylight it receives? _____

_____

_____

_____

4 How much land is at the North Pole? _____

_____

5 Which is warmer, the North Pole or the South Pole? _____

_____

6 Which information about the North Pole did you find most interesting? How would you describe the North Pole to someone who lives in the southern hemisphere? Write a paragraph summarizing what you have learned.

_____

_____

_____

_____

_____

NAME _____ DATE _____

Jack S. Kilby: Inventor of the Microchip

THINK ABOUT THE MATH

- Use multiplication to compare amounts.

- The phrase "*x* times as many" can be rewritten as a multiplication equation.

- Amounts can be compared by saying one amount is *x* times as many as another amount.

- Sometimes an amount cannot be equally divided into groups. We call the amount left over a remainder.

- There are 16 ounces in 1 pound.

- Use estimation to check your answer.

- Use smaller units to define and express larger measurement units.

- Use diagrams that show a scale to show measurement quantities.

Jack S. Kilby's interest in electronics began in high school. His dad had a small electric company in Kansas. After a bad ice storm, Mr. Kilby used amateur radio to help his customers. Fascinated with amateur radio, Jack pursued electrical engineering in college. After college, Jack got a job working for a company that made parts for radios and other communication devices. He took night classes toward a master's degree. Jack said, "Working and going to school at the same time presents some challenges. But it can be done and it's well worth the effort."

At his second job with Texas Instruments, Kilby invented the integrated circuit. It is also known as the microchip. An integrated circuit is an advanced electric circuit. Kilby came up with the idea of combining several parts into one component. He reasoned that all the parts needed for a circuit could be made out of semiconductor material. It can be treated to conduct electricity with positive or negative charges. This process made it possible to make smaller circuits without wires between the parts. One of the first microchips was 11 × 1.5 mm in size. It used germanium, and later models used silicon. Robert Noyce worked on the same ideas at the same time. He invented a similar device that had a different manufacturing process. At the end of it all, scientists agreed that both Kilby and Noyce invented the microchip.

Texas Instruments wanted to sell the general public on the idea of the microchip. In response, Kilby and his co-workers developed the handheld calculator. He went on later in his career to work on the concept of using silicon technology to generate solar power. He was able to continue researching and working on projects most of his life. In 2000, Jack S. Kilby was awarded the Nobel Prize in Physics for his work and contributions to society.

NAME _____ DATE _____

Directions: Think about ways to compare measurements of things as you answer the questions below.

1 In 1961, Kilby and a co-worker built a digital computer for the military. It had 587 integrated circuits. The computer was 6.3 cubic inches. The whole computer weighed 10 ounces.

Rewrite the decimal number that expresses the size of the computer as a mixed number.

Draw a number line to show this measurement.

2 Did the computer weigh more or less than 1 pound? _____ How do you know?

_____

_____

3 The second computer that Texas Instruments built weighed 50 times more than Kilby's computer. About how much did it weigh?

Which unit of measurement would be best to use for this weight? _____

4 The second computer used 14 times more circuits than Kilby's model. How many separate circuits did it have? Round your answer to the nearest hundred.

NAME _____ DATE _____

| Engage | **Directions:** Discuss with classmates what you learned from reading about Jack Kilby. Then, answer the questions below. |

1 What can you tell about Jack Kilby's personality? _____

_____

_____

_____

_____

2 How would you describe Kilby's view on the value of education? _____

_____

_____

_____

_____

3 What feature of the integrated circuit (microchip) led to its success? _____

_____

_____

_____

_____

4 What were Jack Kilby's major contributions to society? _____

_____

_____

_____

_____

5 What award did he receive for his work? _____

_____

NAME _____   DATE _____

Grand Canyon Adventure

Jason bounced in his seat and craned his neck to get a better view. For miles the land had been mostly flat with evergreen trees—not at all what he expected. But now the cliffs of the canyon came into view in the distance beyond the village as they approached.

Everyone said the scenery was magnificent at the Grand Canyon, but Jason also looked forward to the interesting things they would do. While Dad checked into the campground, Jason looked at a brochure. He pointed to a picture of a group of people rafting down a river. "Can we go on a rafting trip?"

"That's why we decided to stay at this campground." Mom smiled. "With the money we save here, we were able to set some money aside to go rafting. In trade, though, I'm counting on a scenic hike." She ruffled Jason's hair. He was too pleased and excited about his home for the next six days to even squirm.

"Did I hear someone planning an itinerary for our vacation?" Dad climbed back in the car and put the campground tag on the dashboard. "One day we should definitely take a drive."

Jason groaned. They had just driven *miles* to get there. A family drive sounded boring to him, but maybe this time looking at the scenery would give him something to do. "Would there be great views so I can take pictures?"

"Yep. It's a good thing cameras are digital now. You can take as many pictures as you like, and it doesn't cost me a thing." Dad grinned and then started whistling as he drove to their campsite.

> **THINK ABOUT THE MATH**
>
> - Think about how accurate your final answer needs to be to determine if you can use estimation to solve a problem.
> - Determine the best thing to do with any remainder left over.
> - Sometimes we round an answer to the nearest whole number that makes sense.
> - A whole number is a multiple of each of its factors.
> - Each whole number is the product of two factors.
> - A prime number has only two factors—one and itself.
> - A composite number has three or more different whole-number factors.
> - Use mental math to see if an answer makes sense.
> - Use division to determine if a number is a multiple of a number.
> - List the factors of a number to determine if a number is prime or composite.
> - Draw pictures to show different ways to solve a problem with combinations of numbers.

NAME _____   DATE _____

Directions: Use information from the passage on page 19 and provided with the questions to solve the problems below.

1 Jason's family planned to take a rafting tour. The guide could take a total of 24 people on the tour. How many families of different sizes could go? List as many possibilities as you can.

2 The day Jason's dad decided to take a drive, they drove from the Visitor Center to see Marble Canyon. The distance one way was 11 miles. Is that distance a prime or composite number?

_____

Show how you know.

3 Jason wanted to buy postcards for his cousin. The price was 2 cards for $1. He had some change in his pocket. What combinations of coins could he use to pay for the postcards?

4 When Jason got home, he had 120 pictures on his camera. How many pictures might he have taken each day if he took the same number each day? Then, show how many pictures he might have taken each day if he took different numbers of pictures on different numbers of days.

NAME _____ DATE _____

Engage **Directions:** Practice working with factors and multiples to solve the problems below.

---

1 Jason's dad thought it would be great to take a drive to see some ruins. The drive was 23 miles one way. They wanted to stop and have lunch on the way to the ruins. Assuming Jason's dad would only drive in whole-mile increments (no fractions of a mile), could they stop for lunch when they are exactly halfway there? Explain why or why not.

_____

_____

If they stop as close to halfway as possible, how far could they drive before and after lunch?

2 The family decided to camp at Mather Campground because it was part of the Grand Canyon Village. They planned to stay 5 nights and the cost was $18 per night. How much would it cost to stay at the campground?

3 The park charges an entrance fee of $30 per car. This fee buys a pass that is good for seven days. How many days did Jason's family stay?

If the fee for the pass is spread out over their visit, what is the cost per day for the park entrance fee?

4 It was a good thing they saved money on the campground because the rafting tour was expensive! The cost was $76 for each child under age 12. Adults 12 and over would pay $86 each. Each person pays a $6 river-use fee. Jason and his sister would be charged the child rate. How much would it cost for the four people in Jason's family to take the half-day raft trip?

How much would they save if Jason's mother decided not to go on the rafting trip?

5 The campground where Jason's family stayed is on the South Rim, at an elevation of 7,000 feet. At the starting point of the raft tour, elevation is 2,400 feet. How far will they go down in elevation to go on the rafting trip?

NAME _____   DATE _____

A Walk Through the Neighborhood

Jeong wrote Evan's address on a piece of paper and shoved it into the pocket of his backpack. "I'll look at a map and my parents will help me find it, no problem. See you tomorrow!" He waved at Evan and walked down the sidewalk in front of the school to where his mom's sedan was parked.

The next morning, he asked Mom about the address. "Evan said he doesn't think it's very far from here, less than a mile."

"Yes, the street where Evan lives is just a few blocks up the hill." Mom sketched a map on the back of Jeong's paper.

Jeong followed along on the map as she talked.

"You know how to get from our house here on Butte Avenue to the youth center on 89th Avenue. There's a bus stop at the corner of the youth center parking lot. Stop and check both ways before crossing Boulder Avenue." Mom gave Jeong an intense look.

"There is more traffic on that street than others in our neighborhood. After you cross the street, keep walking north on 89th Avenue until you get to Mountain Crest Avenue. Turn left and start watching the house numbers."

Jeong put the paper in his pocket and picked up his soccer ball. "I'll call you when I get there!"

He climbed the hill, glad he could catch the bus for his school at the bottom of the hill on days his mom didn't drive him to school. Mom was right; he had to wait for traffic to clear before he could cross Boulder. Just for fun, he read house numbers as he walked along 89th toward Mountain Crest. The numbers were 3-digit numbers and Evan's house number was 4 digits.

Once Jeong got to Mountain Crest, he turned left. The yard of a corner house had been taken over by a jungle of grapes and evergreens. Finally, Jeong could read the numbers on the houses that faced Mountain Crest. He didn't need house numbers when he saw the house that matched Evan's description. The tan house had a huge tree in the front yard and an immaculate porch, except for Evan's bicycle leaning against the railing.

NAME _____ DATE _____

Problem Solving

Directions: Use page 22 to answer these questions. Skim the paragraphs to find information that might help you solve the problem. Remember to show your thinking as you do the math!

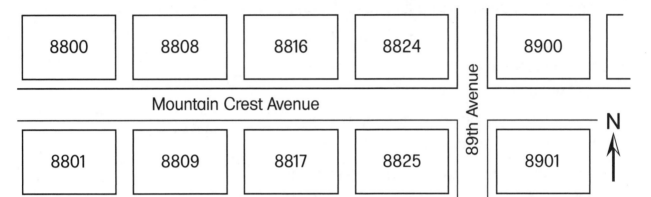

1 What is the rule for house numbering on one side of Evan's street?

2 What is the pattern for the location of even and odd house numbers? _____

_____

Evan's house number is 8817. Is it on the north or south side of the street? _____

3 Is Evan's house east or west of 89th Avenue?

_____

4 What interrupts the pattern of house numbers in the picture? _____

_____

5 Why do you think there are gaps in numbers for house numbers on a street?

_____

_____

_____

_____

NAME _____   DATE _____

Engage

Directions: Use the information given on the previous two pages and below to practice working with number patterns.

- Many cities name north-south streets "Avenue."
- Many cities name east-west streets "Street."
- Often, houses on the north or west side of a street will have even numbers.
- Often, houses on the south or east side of a street will have odd numbers.

- City blocks vary in size, but engineers use a measurement of about 300 feet in length for calculations.
- Often, a city lot has a minimum width of 60 feet.

1 Some house-numbering systems use number increments based on the amount of road-front footage on the property. For instance, in a downtown metropolitan area, house-number increments are based on 15 feet per increment. For two neighboring houses on city lots, what difference would there be in the house numbers? (Assume each city lot is the same minimum width.)

2 What is the maximum amount of houses that would fit along a standard-sized block?

3 What is the house number on your house? _____

What is the number on the house to the right of your house? _____

What is the number on the house to the left of your house? _____

4 What pattern in house numbers have you noticed on your street or in your town? Draw a picture or create a chart to show the pattern.

NAME _____   DATE _____

Freeway Art

Cities are growing larger and becoming more crowded. Government regulations require sound barrier walls in high-traffic areas. At first, the concrete barriers were just that—walls of concrete. In places with temperate climates, some cities planted low-maintenance climbing vegetation, such as varieties of ivy.

Another alternative, which conserves water, is to use concrete that is formed in different designs. This adds a decorative element to the walls and can give each city a distinct personality. The new designs use various textures and other patterns. New technology enables the designs to be cast on both sides of the wall. Commuters and homeowners both benefit from the improved appearance.

Freeway developers also use various colors. Cement blocks come in beige, brown, tan, light tan, red, gray, and sand. Blocks of different colors are put together to form simple patterns. In some parts of the country, many walls have similar appearances. The government builds many of the sound barriers. It is cost effective to use whatever builders keep in stock.

In some places, freeways are constructed lower than the surrounding areas. A freeway will be set in a trench that is roughly a trapezoid shape. Sometimes it only appears that a freeway is set in a trench. It might actually be at the same level as the surrounding neighborhoods. However, huge earth berms act as a natural wall and noise buffer.

Safety is a factor as well. If sound barriers are too interesting, they may distract drivers. Yet a certain break in monotony keeps drivers more alert.

> **THINK ABOUT THE MATH**
> - Patterns often follow a rule.
> - Look for features in a pattern to determine the pattern rule.
> - Use a given rule to identify the next shape in a sequence.
> - Shapes are defined by the number of sides and number and type of angles.
> - Identify the number of angles to name and classify two-dimensional figures.
> - Determine if a two-dimensional figure has parallel and/or perpendicular lines to name and classify the figure.

More communities are looking for ways to add beauty to their cities. At the same time, they have to follow noise-control laws. Adding art to concrete freeway walls accomplishes both purposes.

NAME _____   DATE _____

Directions: Use the information from the passage on page 25 and the pictures below to answer these questions.

1 What repeating shapes do you notice in this freeway sound barrier?

_____

_____

2 How does this structure use vertical and horizontal features to create a pattern?

_____

_____

_____

3 How would you describe the shapes used in this wall?

_____

_____

What mathematical or design rules, if any, does it follow?

_____

How does it meet the goal of being seen and yet not seen, interesting without being too distracting?

_____

_____

_____

_____

NAME _____　　DATE _____

1 Draw a picture of a freeway set below the surrounding area. What do you suppose helps block the freeway noise in this situation?

_____

_____

_____

2 What is one measure that might prevent erosion on sound barriers constructed of earth?

_____

_____

3 What features make an effective design for a sound barrier wall? _____

_____

What shape patterns do you think would help accomplish these things? _____

_____

4 Draw a picture of a concrete wall design you have seen along a freeway or in a picture. What repeating pattern(s) do you notice?

5 Draw a picture of a repeating design of shapes that would make an effective sound barrier along a freeway. Explain why you think it would be effective.

NAME _____   DATE _____

The Transcontinental Railroad

Steam locomotives became widespread in the first half of the 19th century. By 1850, 9,000 miles of track connected cities in the eastern part of the United States. The California Gold Rush of 1849 increased the number of people choosing to travel across country. The overland route was long and dangerous, and many pioneers died in the harsh mountain crossings. A group had become trapped in Donner Pass, part of the Sierra Nevada mountain range, a few years before the Gold Rush.

A young engineer studied Donner Pass and determined it would be a good place to lay railroad track through the mountains. He formed the Central Pacific Railroad Company. Then he went to Washington D.C. to convince the government of the need for a transcontinental railroad. Congress agreed, and President Lincoln signed the Pacific Railroad Act in 1862. The act gave the Central Pacific and Union Pacific Railroad companies the task of building a railroad. It would connect the east and west coasts of the United States. Each company would receive land and up to $48,000 in government bonds for every mile of completed track. The competition began.

Each company met their share of challenges. Native American tribes attacked the Union Pacific, slowing their progress. Natives resented the newcomers taking over their lands. The Central Pacific Railroad faced the challenge of navigating steep mountain passes. The work was so difficult that the company had trouble keeping workers. Finally, Charles Crocker—who was in charge of construction—hired Chinese people to work on the railroad. The number of Chinese workers who worked on the Transcontinental Railroad is estimated to be about 14,000.

The Union Pacific Railroad Company began building in Omaha, Nebraska, and made good progress across the plains at first. The Central Pacific Railroad had its first rails spiked to ties in Sacramento, California. Seven years later, the two railroads met in Promontory, Utah. Crowds cheered and telegraphs flew across the country as the final spike was driven. The Transcontinental Railroad had become a reality!

NAME _____ DATE _____

Problem Solving

Directions: Use page 28 to answer these questions. First, skim the paragraphs to find information that might help you solve the problem. Remember to show your thinking as you do the math!

1 The Central Pacific needed workers. They were hoping for 5,000 workers, but only 200 showed up. What fractional part of the needed labor did they have?

Use what you know about factors and place value to write an equivalent reduced fraction.

Create a visual model to show the amount of labor they had compared to the amount needed.

2 By the time Crocker hired Chinese workers to work on the railroad, there may have been as many as 50,000 Chinese living in California. What fractional part of the Chinese population in California worked for the Central Pacific?

Use what you know about factors to write a reduced equivalent fraction.

3 The longest tunnel built through the Sierras was 1,659 feet long. The workers could blast about 1 foot of rock per day. How many days would it take them to build the tunnel?

How many days are in a year? _____

At that rate, how many years would it take them to build the tunnel? Use rounding to estimate an answer.

NAME _____ DATE _____

Engage | **Directions:** Work together with classmates to solve the problems below and use the information to create additional practice problems.

1 How much land would the Union Pacific receive from the government for the first 40 miles of track laid if the government offered 6,400 acres of land for each mile of the track built? Use place-value strategies and properties of operations to find the amount of land.

2 At first, the Central Pacific laid 350 iron rails, 2,500 wooden ties, and 10,000 spikes for every mile of track. Use expanded notation and place-value strategies to answer these questions:

How many iron rails were needed for every 25 miles of track?

How many wooden ties were needed for every 25 miles of track?

How many spikes were needed for every 25 miles of track?

3 Each company had to build at least 40 miles of usable track before receiving any money from the government.

There were different pay rates.

- $16,000 per mile for flat land
- $32,000 per mile for the high plains
- $48,000 for mountains

How much money did the Union Pacific receive for the first 40 miles of track across the prairie?

30

NAME _____ DATE _____

Amaranth: An Edible Weed

Amaranth is a grain-like plant that is grown in various parts of the world for use as a cereal grain or vegetable. The name means "never fading," which describes this hardy plant well. It has spread around the world and can adapt to low-water conditions. This makes it a valuable food crop in many places. However, it is also resistant to weed-control chemicals.

Cultivated amaranth plants reach a size of 5 to 6 feet. Some plants grow up to 3 inches per day! One variety commonly grown for eating has reddish stems and oval leaves. Its common name is *pigweed*. One species can produce up to one million seeds per plant. One statistic shows that in 2002, ten farms cultivated a total of 939 acres of amaranth. Other estimates suggest as many as 200,000 acres or more were in production. In the United States, it is mostly grown in the Midwest.

Natives in Mexico and South America cultivated amaranth between 6,000 and 8,000 years ago. People in South America still pop amaranth seeds like popcorn today. Sometimes it is mixed with honey for a tasty snack. It is used for traditional breakfast porridge in India, Mexico, and Peru. Native Americans in the United States also use it as a grain. They grind the seeds and make a mush with goat's milk. Ground seeds may be mixed with corn flour and made into bread. The seeds can also be threshed, made into dough, and baked in hot ashes. The greens may be boiled or fried in grease.

Amaranth is not a true grain but has similar nutrients to cereal grains. It is also prepared to be eaten in the same ways as grains. Some species produce thousands of edible seeds, which can be prepared in different ways. The seeds are high in protein and other nutrients. Most importantly for some people, amaranth is a naturally gluten-free food.

> **THINK ABOUT THE MATH**
>
> - A digit in one place represents ten times what it represents in the place to its right.
> - A million is the place value to the left of hundred thousand.
> - We use place value to compare multi-digit numbers.
> - There are 100 years in a century.
> - Say a number aloud to write the words for the number.
> - Use comparison symbols (>, =, and <) to compare two multi-digit numbers.

NAME _____   DATE _____

Problem Solving   **Directions:** Use page 31 to answer these questions. First, skim the paragraphs to find information that might help you solve the problem. Remember to show your thinking as you do the math!

1 Write a number (in word form) to describe how long ago the maximum amount of amaranth was first cultivated.

_____

2 How many centuries ago did people in South America first cultivate amaranth?

3 Write a base-ten numeral to indicate the number of seeds one plant can produce.

_____

4 How many acres of amaranth were cultivated in 2002? _____

If each farm grew the same amount of amaranth, how many acres of amaranth did each farm grow (to the nearest acre)?

5 How many days would it take a fast-growing pigweed plant to reach a height of 6 feet?

6 Write a number sentence (using >, <, or =), comparing the two estimates of amaranth produced in 2002.

NAME _____   DATE _____

Directions: Use the passage on page 31 and other available resources to explore and discuss uses of amaranth with classmates.

1 Why do you think a common name for the plant is *pigweed*? _____

_____

_____

2 Why is this plant a good source of food for people? _____

_____

_____

3 Why might amaranth be a problem for farmers? _____

_____

_____

4 Research to find ways people cook and use amaranth today. Take notes in the box.

5 What do you think would be your favorite way to try eating amaranth? Why?

_____

_____

_____

NAME _____   DATE _____

The Mighty Mississippi

The second longest river in the United States, the "Mighty Mississippi," flows out of Lake Itasca in Minnesota. It empties into the Gulf of Mexico in Louisiana. At the headwaters of the Mississippi River, the water flows a little over one mile per hour. That's one-third as fast as some people walk. By the time the river reaches the delta in New Orleans, the current is three miles per hour.

Rivers constantly change as they flow through channels, and they change the landscape. Different organizations have recorded the length of the Mississippi, and they agree the river is at least 2,300 miles long.

The width of the river changes over its course as well. At the headwaters, it is less than 30 feet across. Although Lake Pepin is a natural lake along the river, it is also part of a pool formed by a lock and dam. As such, it is the widest part of the river that river traffic navigates. This part of the river is almost 2 miles wide.

The depth of the river varies, too. At one point it is 200 feet deep, but in another place, the "Big Muddy" is less than 3 feet deep. The river carries tons of sediment each day.

The river's elevation at Lake Itasca is 1,475 feet, but by the time it reaches the Gulf of Mexico, it has dropped to 0 feet above sea level.

Along the Mississippi River there are 29 locks and dams. Most of the locks are 100 feet wide, which allows double-wide barges to pass through. These man-made structures transformed the river from a series of waterfalls and rapids into a series of pools. This lock and dam system is called the "stairway of water." In places, the dams make the river deeper and wider, but they are not intended to provide flood control.

"Ol' Man River" offers plenty of opportunities for recreation, but its primary use has always been commercial shipping. The "stairway" makes it easier for traffic to navigate the river. The Army Corp of Engineers maintains a 9-foot shipping channel along the river.

NAME _____   DATE _____

Problem Solving   **Directions:** Use page 34 to answer these questions. First, skim the paragraphs to find information that might help you solve the problem. Remember to show your thinking as you do the math!

1 How many times faster does the river flow at its end than at the beginning?

2 How much wider is it at its widest point than at its most narrow part?

3 How many times deeper is the river at its deepest point than at its most shallow?

Round your answer to the nearest ten. _____

4 How many feet in elevation does the river drop from headwaters to gulf? Round your answer to the nearest hundred.

The Empire State Building is 1,454 feet tall. Write a number sentence to compare the height of this famous building with the difference in elevation of the Mississippi River. Then, write a sentence explaining the comparison.

_____

_____

_____

NAME _____ DATE _____

1 What are some of the nicknames for the Mississippi River? _____

_____

Why do you think the river has those names? _____

_____

_____

2 What is the primary use of the river? What are some other ways people use the river?

_____

_____

3 What purpose do the locks and dams along the river serve? _____

_____

How have they changed the river? _____

_____

4 Why is it important to learn about river systems? _____

_____

_____

5 How would you compare the Mississippi River to a river you are familiar with?

_____

_____

6 Research and read literature about the Mississippi River. How do authors describe the river? How do their descriptions differ from factual accounts about the river? What personal connections do you make to the authors' descriptions? Write your responses on the back of this page.

(Possible sources: *Tom Sawyer*, *Adventures of Huckleberry Finn*, *Minn of the Mississippi*, *Swift Rivers*, etc.)

NAME _____   DATE _____

The Gettysburg Address

Four score and seven years ago, our fathers brought forth a new nation. It was born in liberty. The nation was dedicated to the idea that all men are created equal.

Now we are engaged in a great civil war. This war tests the endurance of our nation. Can this country, dedicated to liberty and equality, stand the test? Today we stand on a great battlefield of that war. We have come to dedicate a portion of that field, as a final resting place for those who here gave their lives. Their sacrifice was so our nation might live. It is altogether fitting and proper that we should do this.

We cannot dedicate or consecrate this ground. The brave men who struggled here have already consecrated it. We cannot add or detract from what they have done. The world will not remember what we say here. But it can never forget what they did here. We, the living, should be dedicated to their unfinished work. Those who fought here have thus far nobly advanced the work of freedom. We should dedicate ourselves to the great task remaining before us. From these honored dead we increase our devotion to that cause for which they gave it all. We resolve that they shall not have died in vain. This nation, under God, shall have a new birth of freedom. The government of the people, by the people, for the people, shall not perish from the earth.

THINK ABOUT THE MATH

- A score is 20 years.
- Sometimes we round a number to calculate large amounts.
- A digit in one place represents ten times what it represents in the place to its right.
- Use place-value strategies to work with multi-digit numbers.
- Compose or decompose groups of tens or hundreds to add or subtract multi-digit numbers.
- Use expanded form to decompose and write multi-digit numbers.
- Use what you know about place value to round multi-digit numbers to any place.

Photograph courtesy of the U.S. National Archives and Records Administration, ARC ID 529085.
Abraham Lincoln is framed by the white rectangle.

NAME _____ DATE _____

Problem Solving

Directions: Use page 37 to answer these questions. First, skim the paragraphs to find information that might help you solve the problem. Remember to show your thinking as you do the math!

1 The Gettysburg Address was given in 1863. What year did Lincoln reference at the beginning of his speech? _____

What event that happened in that year does Lincoln reference? _____

_____

2 The Battle of Gettysburg took place July 1–3, 1863. How many years ago did the battle take place?

3 The Union army had 94,000 soldiers and General Lee's army had 72,000. How many more soldiers fought for the North?

4 On the third day, General Lee decided to make an all or nothing attack. He sent 12,500 men with General Pickett. This advance became known as Pickett's charge. Half of Pickett's men were injured or killed. How many men were injured or killed?

Decompose numbers as needed to find the answer.

What fractional amount of his total original army did General Lee send with Pickett? Use estimation and rounding to find the fractional amount in lowest terms.

5 The total number of casualties (injuries or deaths) in the Battle of Gettysberg was 46,000, including 8,000 deaths. How many were injured?

NAME _____　　DATE _____

1 What is one of Lincoln's concerns for the nation in this speech? _____

_____

_____

_____

2 What is one of the American ideals Lincoln connects with the Civil War? _____

_____

_____

_____

3 What was the purpose of the gathering when Lincoln presented the speech?

_____

_____

_____

_____

4 Lincoln says that the gathering will not add or detract from what the soldiers have done, and that the world will not forget what they did. What great act did these soldiers do?

_____

_____

_____

_____

5 What task does Lincoln request his audience complete? _____

_____

_____

_____

NAME _____   DATE _____

The Eagle*

He clasps the crag with crooked hands;

Close to the sun in lonely lands,

Ring'd with the azure world, he stands.

The wrinkled sea beneath him crawls;

He watches from his mountain walls,

And like a thunderbolt he falls.

*by Alfred Lord Tennyson

NAME _____   DATE _____

Problem Solving

Directions: Answer the following questions using the information provided in each problem.

1. Golden eagles dive toward prey at speeds of more than 150 miles per hour. How many miles per minute do they dive?

2. Red-tailed hawks dive at a speed of 120 miles per hour. How many miles per minute do they dive?

3. The poet says the eagle falls "like a thunderbolt." A thunderbolt is like a bolt of lightning; the heat from the lightning makes the sound of thunder.

   The sound of thunder travels at about 760 miles per hour. How many miles per minute does it travel to the nearest whole mile?

4. Write a number sentence to compare the golden eagle's dive to the dive of the red-tailed hawk.

   Write a number sentence to compare the golden eagle's dive to the speed at which the sound of thunder travels.

5. Research to learn the speeds at which other birds dive for prey. On a separate sheet of paper, create a chart to compare the dive speeds in miles per hour and miles per minute. Alternatively, create a chart of speeds at which various birds fly in level flight.

NAME _____   DATE _____

1 What do you notice about the words in the first line? _____

_____

How does this set the tone for the poem? _____

_____

2 What literary devices does the poet use in the second line? _____

_____

3 Which words in the poem paint a visual picture for the reader? _____

_____

Write a paragraph in your own words to describe this scene. _____

_____

_____

_____

4 What message is the poet trying to convey to the reader in this poem?

_____

_____

5 Think of your favorite animal. Write some words to describe that animal.

_____

Which feature stands out to you the most about that animal? _____

_____

What would you like to say to someone about the animal? _____

_____

On a separate sheet of paper, use your notes to write a poem describing a unique feature of your favorite animal. Illustrate your poem and share with classmates.

NAME _____   DATE _____

Montana Sapphires

Over 150 years ago, the first United States sapphires were discovered in the gravel of the Missouri River in Montana. They were identified as igneous in nature.

Scientists classify minerals by their characteristics, such as hardness, clarity, and color. Sapphires from Yogo Gulch in Montana are unique. They have unusual clarity for a sapphire. They have a natural cornflower blue color. In their natural form, they are small and flat, which means the stones are often too small to cut. It is unusual to find a Yogo sapphire over 1 carat in size.

Yogo Gulch mine is in central Montana, about 78 miles southeast of Great Falls. At one point, the Yogo mine is 61 m deep. Several dikes, or fissures, have been found in that area. The main dike, Dike A, has the most mining activity.

Sapphires are mined from other areas in Montana, but they are not as valuable. Stones from the Missouri River have round, smooth surfaces. In contrast, stones from Rock Creek have a hexagon shape. Both mine locations produce stones that are often pale blue or blue-green in color. Some stones are other pastel colors, such as green, pink, red, purple, yellow, or orange. Most of the stones are less than 1 cm in diameter.

Montana sapphires have industrial uses as well, such as in instrument bearings. In recent times, synthetic sapphires have replaced natural stones for these uses. Today, most sapphires are sold as gemstones so people can appreciate and enjoy their beauty.

THINK ABOUT THE MATH

- Compose groups of tens or hundreds to add or subtract multi-digit numbers.
- Use properties of operations and place-value strategies to multiply or divide multi-digit numbers.
- A carat is a unit of weight equal to 200 mg.
- There are 1,000 g in 1 kg.
- There are 1,000 mg in 1 g.
- There are 100 cm in 1 m.
- Use a visual fraction model to show that $\frac{a}{b}$ is equivalent to $\frac{(n \times a)}{(n \times b)}$.
- Use what you know about powers of 10 to create equivalent fractions.
- Use smaller units to express and define larger measurement units.

NAME _____   DATE _____

Directions: Use page 43 to answer these questions. First, skim the paragraphs to find information that might help you solve the problem. Remember to show your thinking as you do the math!

1 A stone that weighs 1 kg would be equal to how many grams? _____

How many mg would that same stone be equal to? _____

How many carats would that stone be equal to? _____

What fractional part of 1 g is 1 carat? _____

2 Individual stones have been found at the mine weighing as much as 12 carats. What is the weight in mg of such a stone?

What is the weight in grams? _____

3 What is the diameter of many sapphires found in Montana? _____

Draw a picture to show the size of most sapphires.

4 How many centimeters deep is the Yogo mine? _____

5 In mining terms, a vertical fissure formed by igneous rock is referred to as a *dike*. The main dike, Dike A, at Yogo Gulch is 2.4 m wide and 5 km long. Another smaller dike, Dike D, is no more than 1.2 m wide and 152 m long.

How many times wider is Dike A than Dike D?

NAME _____   DATE _____

> **Engage**
>
> **Directions:** Look back at the passage on page 43 to explore and learn more about Montana sapphires. Then, answer the questions below.

1 Based on the text, what approximate date
was the Yogo Gulch mine deposit discovered? _____

2 What type of minerals are the Montana sapphires? _____

3 One way scientists classify minerals is by hardness. If sapphires have industrial uses, what does this tell you about where they might fall on the hardness scale?

_____

_____

4 What does *synthetic* mean? Why do you suppose the industry now uses synthetic sapphires?

_____

_____

_____

5 What shape is a sapphire found in Rock Creek?

_____

Draw a picture of such a stone.

6 What else would you like to learn about sapphires? Why? Where could you find this information?

_____

_____

_____

_____

NAME _____ DATE _____

Razor Clams

Nothing tastes better on a cold, windy day at the beach than a bowl of steaming clam chowder! Pacific razor clams are a meaty shellfish native to the western coast of the United States. They grow up to 6 inches in length, although most that are dug are smaller.

Their main habitat is in the sand of beaches that are exposed at low tide. Southwest Washington has several such beaches. There is also a stable clam population in northwest Oregon. People dig for other varieties of clams on the Atlantic coast.

"Clamming," or digging for razor clams, has become a popular hobby. When the tides are right and there is good weather, as many as a thousand people per mile might dig. In one year alone, close to 300,000 people went to the beach to dig clams. Often, a single person will make more than one trip to dig clams.

The total number of clams harvested in recent years has decreased. Disease and over-harvesting plays a role in the total clam population. Occasionally, clam digging will be prohibited during times when toxins are found in the clams.

Clam digging requires very little equipment. All a person needs is a shovel, a container, and a license. Sometimes low tides happen at night. A few people brave the weather and darkness and take lanterns or flashlights to dig in the dark. Most people wait for good weather and daylight low tides.

NAME _____ DATE _____

Problem Solving

Directions: Use page 46 to answer these questions. First, skim the paragraphs to find information that might help you solve the problem. Remember to show your thinking as you do the math!

1 One year, people made 650,000 trips to the beach to dig clams. If each person made 2 trips, how many people went clam digging?

2 People can only keep the first 15 clams they dig each day; that is their limit for the day. The group Alison is clamming with has 60 clams at the end of the day. How many people went clamming with Alison if each person has their daily limit?

3 If James goes clamming for 3 days on a long weekend, how many clams might he bring home? (Use information from question 2 in your calculations.)

4 One thousand people can dig clams on a mile of beach. It is 15 miles from Long Beach to Willapa Bay, a section of beach identified as a good area for clamming. On a crowded weekend, how many people might clam along this stretch of beach?

If there are 1,000 people in a mile of beach, how much width space does each clam digger have to the nearest foot?

5 West Coast clams dig downward one foot every 30 seconds. It's been over a minute since you saw the place to dig. How deep might the clam be by now?

_____

If a digger finds a clam 3 feet deep, how long has it been since the clam was at the surface?

_____

NAME _____   DATE _____

Directions: Answer the questions to practice problem solving and learn more about razor clams on the East Coast.

1 Atlantic razor clams are 5–9 inches long. They are about 6 times longer than wide.

About how wide is the largest Atlantic razor clam? Express any remainder as a fraction.

2 The foot—a clam's only appendage—can extend to one half the length of the body. How far can the foot extend? Solve for a 5 in. clam and a 9 in. clam.

Draw a number line. Mark the number line to show how far the foot can extend for each common length of clam (5–9").

3 Atlantic razor clams dig into the sand at a rate of 12 inches every half minute. How does this compare with the speed at which razor clams on the West Coast (see page 47) dig into the sand? Write a number sentence to compare the speeds.

4 Researchers are working to develop a robot that can dig in the sand in a way similar to a razor clam. The fascination is that the razor clam digs quickly with very little energy—about the amount needed by a AA battery. What tasks could such a device accomplish?

_____

_____

_____

NAME _____   DATE _____

China's Ghost City

The city of Ordos, China is a wealthy coal-mining town in Inner Mongolia. One part of the city in particular has gained attention as a modern "ghost town." The Kangbashi district was designed to have a population of one million, which is roughly the size of San Diego, California. Today, hardly anyone lives there.

This urban district has office buildings and duplexes. It has sports fields and government buildings. There is a public library and a modern museum. Photos show streets of empty houses, and apartment buildings stand mostly vacant. Commercial complexes are also mostly empty; almost no businesses have moved into the district. As a result, there's not enough traffic to create congestion at rush hour.

What created this deserted urban landscape? Over a decade ago, a large coal deposit was discovered. Mining began, which generated wealth. When there is money, people will build. The government encouraged people to move to the new district. Government offices and schools were moved to the new area.

Prior to the discovery of coal, the area's main industry was wool and textiles. It was one of the poorer regions of China. Incomes have increased, and there are plans to connect the "old city" with the new district to create one large metropolitan area. On a recent visit to the city, a reporter observed a positive attitude of hope, as the city comes to life.

THINK ABOUT THE MATH

- Compose groups of tens or hundreds to add or subtract multi-digit numbers.

- A fraction with a denominator that is a power of 10 can be written as a decimal number. For example, $\frac{6}{10} = .6$ and $\frac{17}{100} = .17$.

- Use place-value strategies and properties of operations to multiply or divide multi-digit numbers.

- Use what you know about place value to round multi-digit numbers to any place.

- Use a visual fraction model to show the fractional amount of something.

Photograph by Uday Phalgun, CC BY 2.0.

NAME _____ DATE _____

Problem Solving   **Directions:** Use page 49 to answer these questions. First, skim the paragraphs to find information that might help you solve the problem. Remember to show your thinking as you do the math!

1 The coal reserves discovered in the area represent $\frac{1}{6}$ of the country's total coal resources. Draw a diagram to show how much of the coal in China is found in the Ordos region.

2 Recent reports estimate the city's population at 100,000 people. What fractional part of the original 1,000,000 is that? Use place value and division to create a smaller equivalent fraction.

3 Early in the period of increased economic growth, farmers and small businessmen sold land to mining enterprises and developers. In one case, a banker invested in property and paid the former landholder $9,584 over a two-year period.

How much did the landowner receive each year?

Round to the nearest hundred. _____

4 One landowner started with $11,980. Half of his money disappeared when one of the bankers fled the area, taking the landowner's money with him. How much money did the landowner lose?

Round the amount to the nearest thousand. _____

NAME _____ DATE _____

Engage | **Directions:** Work with a small group of classmates to design and plan a model for a city.

---

1 Draw and label a picture of your city plan.

```
[blank box for drawing]
```

2 Use information from your city plan to create and answer math-related questions about your city.

Examples:

- How many square miles is the area of your city?
- How many people will live in your city?
- How many people per square mile will your city support?
- What is the price of a house?
- How many square feet does a house have?
- What is the housing price per square foot?
- Include information about wages, number of different types of buildings, streets, etc.

3 Use the data generated from your group's questions and answers to create a brochure advertising your city. Use another sheet of paper to complete this activity.

4 Present your city to other small groups in your class.

NAME _____   DATE _____

Pumpkin Bars

"Is the pumpkin defrosted, Mom?" Benjamin set the flour and the oil on the counter.

Mom handed him the recipe card. "I think so. What other ingredients do you need?"

He read the card, and then reached into the refrigerator for butter and carrots. "Should I use one egg or two?"

"Use two. Do you want to put the bars in a square pan or a round pan?"

Benjamin stopped, an egg in each hand. "I might get more bars in two round pans but the pieces would be easier to cut in a square pan. I'll figure it out in a minute." He set the eggs on the counter and pulled out a large metal bowl. Propping the recipe up where he could see it, Benjamin started adding ingredients to the bowl.

After the pumpkin bars came out of the oven, Benjamin had a tough choice. He could share them with his family or with his friends at the soccer game the next day.

Pumpkin Carrot Bars

1. Blend together:
   - 2 eggs
   - $\frac{1}{2}$ cup brown sugar
   - $\frac{1}{2}$ cup pumpkin
   - 2 Tablespoons oil
   - 2 Tablespoons melted butter
   - 1 Tablespoon grated orange rind

2. Combine dry ingredients and blend into wet mixture:
   - 1 cup flour (option: use half whole-wheat flour)
   - 1 teaspoon baking powder
   - $\frac{1}{2}$ teaspoon cinnamon
   - $\frac{1}{4}$ teaspoon baking soda
   - $\frac{1}{4}$ teaspoon salt
   - $\frac{1}{4}$ teaspoon cloves

3. Stir in:
   - $\frac{3}{4}$ cup raisins
   - $\frac{1}{2}$ cup grated carrot

4. Pour into a square pan or two small round pans. Bake at 350 degrees for 25 minutes.

Optional: Sprinkle powdered sugar over the top or make a glaze with cream cheese, butter, vanilla, and a little powdered sugar.

NAME _____   DATE _____

Directions: Use page 52 to answer these questions. First, skim the paragraphs and the recipe to find information that might help you solve the problem. Remember to show your thinking as you do the math!

1 The recipe called for $\frac{1}{2}$ cup of pumpkin. Benjamin could only find a one-quarter cup for measuring. How many times would he need to fill the $\frac{1}{4}$ cup to have the right amount of pumpkin?

Write an equation to prove your answer is correct.

2 Benjamin put the batter into 1 large round pan. After it was done baking, he cut the bars so there were 8 pieces. If there were 2 pieces left the next morning, what fraction of the bars were eaten by Benjamin's family?

Use a visual model to show how much was eaten.

3 The recipe calls for $\frac{3}{4}$ cup of raisins. If Benjamin wanted to cut the recipe in half, how many cups of raisins would he use? Use a visual fraction model to solve.

4 The next time he made pumpkin bars he decided to put them in a square pan. He cut the bars into 9 square pieces. Draw a visual model to show how he cut the bars.

Ben wrapped up 3 bars to share with friends at the soccer game Saturday. How many bars are left over? What fraction of the bars are left in the pan?

NAME _____   DATE _____

> **Engage** | **Directions:** Use page 52 to answer the questions below. Think about the main idea and details of what you read.

1 Compare the amount of cinnamon and cloves used in the recipe. Write a number sentence to show which spice has a greater amount.

2 What might happen if Benjamin put the bars into 2 round pans? _____

_____

_____

3 What does *optional* mean? _____

_____

_____

4 Do you think you would like pumpkin bars better with or without the optional topping? Explain your answer.

_____

_____

_____

5 Which food have you had that is most like this recipe? When have you had that food? Write a paragraph about your experience.

_____

_____

_____

_____

_____

NAME _____ DATE _____

Arena Football

Arena football is played in an indoor arena. The sport first became a recognized national sport in 1987. Six years earlier, James Foster was watching an indoor soccer game. His sketch of a football field over an ice hockey diagram formed the foundation for arena football. The first test game was played in 1986. The positive response led to a showcase game played a year later in Chicago.

An indoor arena is smaller than an outdoor football field. The playing field is 50 yards long with an 8-yard end zone at each end. The field is 85 feet wide. Goal posts stand at the ends of the field with a net on either side of the goal posts.

Each team has a roster of 20 active players and 4 inactive players. The offensive team has 8 players on the field. Four players may be on the line of scrimmage. The defensive team also has 8 players on the field. Three players must be down linemen. Originally, rules limited players from coming onto and off the field. As a result, some players would play both offensive and defensive positions. This type of player is referred to as an "ironman." These rules have been changed, however.

One offensive player may go into motion before the ball is snapped at kickoff. Kickoff occurs from an end zone. The offensive team has 4 "downs," or tries to advance the ball 10 yards or to score. Teams score points for touchdowns and field goals.

THINK ABOUT THE MATH

- There are 3 feet in 1 yard.
- $n \times (\frac{a}{b}) = \frac{(n \times a)}{b}$
- A fraction $\frac{a}{b}$ is equivalent to a fraction $\frac{(n \times a)}{(n \times b)}$.
- Use a visual fraction model to explain equivalent fractions.
- A visual fraction model is a tape diagram, number-line diagram, or an area model.
- In visual fraction models, the number and size of parts may differ even though two fractions represent the same overall part of the whole.
- Use factors and multiples to create common denominators to compare fractions.
- A fraction $\frac{a}{b}$ is a multiple of $\frac{1}{b}$.
- Find the area of a rectangle by multiplying the width by the length.
- Use expanded notation to multiply two multi-digit numbers.

NAME _____ DATE _____

Directions: Use page 55 to answer these questions. First, skim the paragraphs to find information that might help you solve the problem. Remember to show your thinking as you do the math!

1 An outdoor NFL football field is 100 yards long with an additional 10 yards for each end zone. Not including the end zones, what fraction best describes the relationship of the length of the arena football field compared to the NFL football field?

Draw and label a diagram to prove your answer.

2 Write a fraction to compare the size of an end zone in arena football to an end zone in NFL football. _____

3 What is the area of the arena football playing field, excluding the end zones, in square feet?

4 What fraction of the total playing field must the offense advance to maintain possession of the ball by the 4th down?

_____

Use what you know about multiples of 10 to write an equivalent fraction.

_____

Draw a diagram to show the fraction of the field the offensive team must gain to maintain possession of the ball.

5 What fraction of the total number of active players are on the field at a time? _____

Use what you know about factors to write equivalent fractions.

_____

Draw a visual fraction model to show the fraction of players in active play.

NAME _____   DATE _____

Engage   **Directions:** Research to learn more about the differences between arena football and outdoor NFL football. Alternatively, compare arena football with a sport you know and enjoy.

1 Work with classmates to create a T-chart to list the differences between arena football and outdoor NFL football. Alternatively, express the similarities and differences in a Venn diagram.

2 Use your notes from question 1 to write a compare-and-contrast paragraph.

_____

_____

_____

_____

_____

_____

3 Write a second paragraph expressing your preference for one game over the other. Include details, examples, and reasons to support your argument. Present your paragraph to classmates.

_____

_____

_____

_____

_____

_____

NAME _____   DATE _____

Hummingbirds

Hummingbirds fly in all directions, including right or left, up or down. They can even fly upside down! Hummingbirds flap their wings about 50 times every second. This is so fast, all we see is a blur.

They use their tiny feet to perch on small branches. If they want to travel more than two inches, they must fly. Before they lift off, they flap their wings at almost full speed. They fly fast but can stop suddenly. Hummingbirds don't weigh much, which enables them to also make quick landings.

Because hummingbirds are in almost constant motion, they need to eat a lot. They feed every 10 minutes or so and eat two-thirds of their body weight each day. These tiny birds eat sugar from flower nectar, as well as small insects and pollen. The sugar gives them energy. Insects provide protein, which helps build strong wing muscles. Their long bill helps them get nectar from flowers. They have long tongues, too, to lick the nectar.

Males will fight to protect a food source. They fight less when food is scarce. Females guard their nests and feed the young.

Hummingbirds fly south for the winter, with some species traveling as far south as Mexico. Others go only as far as the Gulf of Mexico. In the spring, they migrate north. They may go as far north as Canada.

One small bird cannot be seen by predators, so hummingbirds do not migrate in flocks. They fly low in search of food along the way.

It takes one to four weeks for a bird to migrate, traveling 20 to 25 miles per day. They stop for food and rest and sleep at night. Some species travel farther than others. They store up to half their body weight before they migrate.

People study hummingbirds to learn more about flight. They learn how these amazing birds do the things they do.

NAME _____   DATE _____

Problem Solving   **Directions:** Use page 58 to answer these questions. First, skim the paragraphs to find information that might help you solve the problem. Remember to show your thinking as you do the math!

1 About how many times do hummingbirds flap their wings in 5 minutes? _____

_____

2 How much food per day do hummingbirds usually eat? _____

One common species of hummingbird weighs 3 grams. What would be two-thirds of its body weight? Write and simplify an expression with a fraction.

3 Before they migrate, hummingbirds store up to half of their body weight.

How much does the hummingbird from question 2 weigh? _____

How much food would be half of its body weight? Write an expression with a fraction. Simplify and convert your answer to a mixed number.

4 If it takes a hummingbird 4 weeks to migrate at 23 miles per day, how many miles does it travel?

5 To find the greatest distance a hummingbird might migrate, answer the questions below.

What is the longest migration time (in days)? _____

What is the greatest number of miles a hummingbird might fly in one day?

_____

Write an equation using expanded form to find the greatest total distance.

NAME _____   DATE _____

> **Engage**   **Directions:** Answer the questions below.

1 Why do people study hummingbirds to learn about flight? _____

_____

_____

2 How have people applied what they have observed in hummingbird behavior to human flight?

_____

_____

_____

3 What do hummingbirds eat? How do these foods help them? _____

_____

_____

_____

4 What else do you think people can learn from studying hummingbirds?

_____

_____

_____

_____

_____

_____

_____

NAME _____   DATE _____

Troy's Spaghetti Sauce

Troy arranged the cans on the counter next to the crockpot. "That's a lot of cans to open," he said as he picked up the can opener.

"After you put the cans of sauce in, add the olive oil, then the meat." Mom set a colander with cooked hamburger and ground sausage on a plate to drain. "By then it will be cool enough, but you'll have to use both hands to pour the meat from the colander."

He spooned tomato sauce and tomato paste from the opened cans into the crockpot. "Did you already chop the vegetables?"

Mom pointed to the cutting board. "Yes, add them after the meat." She washed and dried her hands on a kitchen towel.

After he emptied the cans, Troy put them in the sink to rinse for recycling. He carefully picked up the colander and held it over the crockpot. "Mom, can you spoon the meat in? I don't have enough hands!"

"This already smells great, and the vegetables and spices aren't even in yet!" Troy scooped the chopped vegetables into a bowl to carry them to the counter where he was working. He held the bowl with one hand and spooned chopped onion, green pepper, garlic, and mushrooms into the sauce.

Mom had set spices and measuring spoons out on the counter. Troy consulted the recipe and added chili powder, oregano, and Italian seasoning to the mixture. Last, he poured $1\frac{1}{2}$ cups water over the top of it all.

THINK ABOUT THE MATH

- Each whole number is the product of two or more factors.
- A mixed number can be replaced with an equivalent fraction after it is converted to an improper fraction.
- There are 16 ounces in 1 pound.
- There are 8 fluid ounces in 1 cup.
- Use division to determine if a number is a multiple of another number.
- To add or subtract mixed numbers with like denominators, add the fractions, regroup any improper fractions to whole numbers, and then add the whole numbers.

Spaghetti Sauce

- 2 T. olive oil
- 1 large onion, chopped
- $\frac{1}{2}$ of a green pepper, chopped
- 2 cloves garlic, chopped
- 2 mushrooms, sliced
- $\frac{1}{2}$ pound ground beef, cooked
- $\frac{1}{2}$ pound sausage, cooked

- 29 ounces tomato sauce
- 12 ounces tomato paste
- 1 teaspoon chili powder
- 1 teaspoon oregano
- 1 teaspoon Italian seasoning
- $1\frac{1}{2}$ cups water

Simmer in crockpot 3–5 hours. Stir occasionally.

NAME _____   DATE _____

Directions: Use page 61 to answer these questions. First, skim the paragraphs and the recipe to find information that might help you solve the problem. Remember to show your thinking as you do the math!

1 How many cups of tomato sauce does the recipe call for?

2 How many cups of tomato paste does the recipe call for?

3 Given the amount of water, tomato sauce, and tomato paste, about how many cups of sauce will Troy make?

_____

Use mixed numbers to add the ingredient amounts.

4 Troy added meat and vegetables to the spaghetti sauce. Altogether, he added about 2 cups of meat, $1\frac{1}{2}$ cups chopped onion, $\frac{1}{2}$ cup chopped green pepper, and $\frac{1}{2}$ cup chopped mushrooms. The garlic and spices are in much smaller amounts and mostly add flavor. After the spaghetti sauce is cooked, about how many cups of sauce did Troy have?

5 One serving is $\frac{1}{2}$ cup of spaghetti sauce. About how many $\frac{1}{2}$-cup servings did Troy make? Draw a visual fraction model to solve.

6 About how many ounces of sauce did Troy make in all?

NAME _____   DATE _____

Engage   **Directions:** Think about the passage on page 61. Then, answer the questions below.

1 What difference might the order in which ingredients are added make? _____

_____

_____

2 Why did Troy have to hold the colander with both hands? _____

_____

3 Why do you suppose the sauce cooks for several hours? _____

_____

_____

4 What other ingredients might someone add to spaghetti sauce? If possible, research ingredients people from other cultures use in a similar meat sauce.

_____

_____

_____

5 What are some ways to use this spaghetti sauce once it is cooked? _____

_____

_____

_____

6 What are your favorite ingredients to include in spaghetti sauce? _____

_____

_____

_____

NAME _____   DATE _____

Wilma Rudolph: Overcoming to Win

When Wilma Rudolph was born, no one could have guessed she would grow up to be an Olympic champion. She was born early and underweight to a poor family in Tennessee. Polio and pneumonia left her disabled for most of her childhood. After polio paralyzed her left leg, doctors said she would never walk again. Family members massaged her legs every day, and she wore a brace for many years.

Wilma learned to walk again. By the time she was 12, she was playing basketball. When a university track coach saw her, he thought she had potential. She trained with him during the summers and won several races at high school track meets.

A year later, Wilma attended her first Olympic Games, which were held in Australia in 1956. Her 4 × 100-meter relay team took bronze that year. After high school she went to Tennessee State University as a member of the track team. She worked hard and made the Olympic team along with three other members of the track team.

They went to Rome for the 1960 Olympic Games. Wilma won gold medals in the 100-meter race and the 200-meter race. She was on the team that won gold in the 400-meter relay with a time of $44\frac{5}{10}$ seconds. Her times matched or broke 3 world records. She became the first woman to win 3 gold medals in track and field in a single Olympic Games.

After her Olympic Games championship, Rudolph retired from professional athletics. She went on to teach, coach, and work with underprivileged children.

NAME _____   DATE _____

Problem Solving

Directions: Use what you know about working with fractions to answer the questions below. Remember to show your thinking as you do the math!

1 Four people are on a 400-meter relay team. How far does each person run? _____

What fractional amount of the race does each team member run? _____

Use a visual model to find the fractional amount.

2 Wilma ran the 100-meter race in 11 seconds. The silver medal went to Dorothy Hyman from Great Britain. She ran the race in $11\frac{3}{10}$ seconds.

Rewrite the silver medalist's time with a denominator of 100. _____

3 Four years later, at the 1964 Olympic Games in Tokyo, the gold medal winner for the 100-meter race had a time of $11\frac{4}{10}$ seconds.

Write a number sentence to compare this time with Wilma Rudolph's time.

What is the difference between the two race times?

4 Wilma also ran the 200-meter race. How many times longer is this race than the 100-meter race?

_____

Based on her speed in the 100-meter race, estimate her time in the 200-meter race. _____

5 Wilma's 4 × 100 team won the relay in $44\frac{5}{10}$ seconds. The second place team had a time of $44\frac{8}{10}$ seconds. How much faster was the winning team?

_____

Write the winning time as a decimal number. _____

6 The gold medal 400-meter relay team in the 1964 Olympic Games had a time of $43\frac{6}{10}$ seconds. Write an equation to show the difference between the time of Wilma's team in 1960 and the 1964 team.

Which team had the faster time? _____

NAME _____   DATE _____

Engage   **Directions:** Refer to the passage on page 64 and discuss with classmates what makes Wilma Rudolph an overcomer.

1 What challenge did Wilma face early in life? _____

_____

_____

2 What helped Wilma overcome her challenge? _____

_____

_____

3 What were Wilma's early experiences in sports? _____

_____

_____

4 How would you describe Wilma's Olympic Games experience(s)? _____

_____

_____

_____

_____

_____

5 How did Wilma use her early experiences later in life? _____

_____

_____

_____

_____

_____

NAME _____   DATE _____

John Napier: The Decimal Point

John Napier was born into a nobleman's family in Scotland. He did not attend formal school during his early years, as was the custom. Within a few years, he left and went to England for more education.

John Napier encouraged others to adopt the decimal point system. Other mathematicians had worked on such a system. Napier built upon earlier research. It said a simple point could be used to separate a whole number from fractional parts of the number.

Astronomers of the time calculated the movements of planets and stars. This required many long computations. Napier had an interest in astronomy and spent years working with the calculations. He understood that large numbers can be expressed in different ways. This led him to come up with better and faster ways to work with numbers.

He also invented new ways to compute the answers to math problems. We use a form of that today when we use a series of steps to solve similar problems. One example is multiplying or dividing multi-digit numbers.

Today Napier is best known for his work in mathematics and astronomy. He even has a crater on the moon named after him!

THINK ABOUT THE MATH

- A fraction whose denominator is a power of 10 can be written as a decimal number. For example, $\frac{6}{10} = .6$ and $\frac{17}{100} = .17$.

- Find the perimeter of a rectangle by adding the length to the width and multiplying the result by 2.
$P = 2(l + w)$

- Use visual models to determine fractional amounts of a whole.

- Use a diagram to justify a calculation for perimeter of a rectangle.

NAME _____   DATE _____

Directions: Use page 67 to answer these questions. First, skim the paragraphs to find information that might help you solve the problem. Remember to show your thinking as you do the math!

1 John Napier's first wife died, leaving him with two children. He married again, and had ten children by his second wife. Five of them were sons.

Write a fraction to show how many of his children by his second wife were boys. _____

Express this as a decimal. _____

2 Napier experimented with using manure to fertilize his crops. Perhaps he tried it on 7 plots out of 10.

Draw a picture to show these fields and write the number of fields in which he experimented with manure as a fraction.

Express this number as a decimal. _____

3 Some people told a story about John Napier because they thought he didn't trust his workers. It was said that his tools and supplies kept disappearing. He questioned his workers, but no one confessed. One day, he gathered the workers and told them his rooster could tell who was telling the truth. John had each person go in, pet the rooster, and come back out. After everyone had gone in the shed, Napier looked at their hands. All but one had black palms. He had put lamp black (soot) on his rooster. The guilty man was afraid to pet the rooster and his hands were clean.

If there were 10 workers, what fractional part of the workers had clean hands? _____

If there were 100 workers, what fractional part of the workers had clean hands? _____

4 Write one or more decimal problems for a classmate to solve.

NAME _____   DATE _____

1 How do we use decimal points today? _____

_____

_____

2 What are some quantities that we express in tenths or hundredths? _____

_____

_____

3 One inch equals 2.54 cm. Write this centimeter measurement using a fraction. _____

4 What is the width in inches of this page? Write
the measurement as a fraction and a decimal. _____

What is the width in centimeters? Write your answer as a decimal. _____

5 What is the length in inches of this page? _____

What is the length in centimeters? Write your answer as a decimal. _____

6 What is the perimeter of this page in centimeters? _____

Write and solve an equation to prove your answer is correct.

NAME _____   DATE _____

Buckets of Rain

Scientists measure rainfall in hundredths of an inch. Weather records were set in the Pacific Northwest in August 2014. On August 13, a record was set for the amount of rain in a 24-hour period. It rained 6.43 inches. The previous record for the date was 2.38. That record was set in 2004. The average daily rainfall for that date is less than one half inch.

Sometimes drastic weather changes occur in a short time period. Later in August, the warmest day of 2014 was recorded in the Pacific Northwest. The temperature reached 88 degrees that day. The year of 2014 did not have any days that reached 90 degrees in that area. In an average year in the Pacific Northwest, there are five 90-degree days in August. Overall, though, the average temperature for the month was a couple of degrees above normal. August also had more warm nights than usual.

NAME _____ DATE _____

Problem Solving **Directions:** Use page 70 to answer these questions. First, skim the paragraphs to find information that might help you solve the problem. Remember to show your thinking as you do the math!

1 Which whole number most closely represents the record amount of rainfall on August 13, 2014? _____

What is the decimal number that expresses the exact amount of rain that fell? _____

Write that number as a mixed number. _____

2 Which whole number most closely represents the record amount of rainfall on that same date in 2004? _____

What is the decimal number that expresses the exact amount of rain that fell? _____

Write that number as a mixed number. _____

3 Which year had the higher record amount of rainfall, 2004 or 2014?

_____

Write a comparison statement to prove your answer.

4 How much greater was the amount of rainfall recorded in 2014 than the previous record for that date?

5 The month with the second highest amount of rainfall during 2014 was March. In that month 6.14 inches of rain fell.

Draw a number-line diagram to compare the amount of rain that fell during the month of March with the amount that fell on one day, August 13, of that same year.

Write a comparison statement to compare the amounts.

What is the difference in the amount of rain that fell during those two time periods?

NAME _____   **DATE** _____

Engage   **Directions:** Research to learn more about weather patterns in your town. Use almanacs, local newspapers, weather reports, or Internet sources. Use what you learn to write math problems for classmates.

1 Find rainfall or temperature weather records for your area and compare recorded highs to the amount in the current year.

2 Compare the rainfall on two or more days during the year. Show the amounts on a number-line diagram.

3 Write problems about the weather for classmates to solve. Consider writing problems about decimal notation of rainfall amounts, asking about the fraction of days in a month with rainfall, or writing comparison problems.

NAME _____   DATE _____

Paul Bunyan*

Have you ever encountered the Mosquito of the North Country? If so, then you probably thought they had pretty good appetites, and you can appreciate what Paul Bunyan was up against when he was surrounded by vast swarms of the insects. He saw giant ancestors of the present race of mosquitoes. They were getting their first taste of human victims. The mosquitoes today are only a remnant of the species. Now they rarely weigh more than 450 grams or measure more than 35 to 38 cm from tip to tip.

Paul had to keep his men and oxen in the camps with doors and windows barred. Men armed with pike-poles and axes fought off mosquitoes. The insects tore the shakes (wooden shingles) off the roof to get inside. The big buck mosquitoes fought among themselves and trampled down the weaker members of the swarm.

Paul was determined to conquer the mosquitoes before another season arrived. He sent for several yoke of the big bumblebees back home, hoping they would destroy the mosquitoes. Sourdough Sam brought two pairs of the bees to Paul. He walked them on foot over the land. There was no other way to travel, for the flight of the beasts could not be controlled. Their wings were strapped, and they checked their stingers with Sam. Sam gave them walking shoes and brought them through without losing a bee.

The cure was worse than the original trouble. The mosquitoes and the bees were a hit with each other. They soon intermarried. Their offspring, as often happens, were worse than their parents. They had stingers before and behind and could get you coming or going.

Their bee blood caused their downfall in the long run. Their craving for sweets could only be satisfied by sugar and molasses in large amounts. What is a flower to an insect with a 40-liter stomach?

One day, the whole tribe flew across Lake Superior to attack a fleet of ships bringing sugar to Paul's camps. They destroyed the ships but ate so much sugar, they could not fly and all were drowned.

One pair of the original bees was kept at headquarters camp. They provided honey for the pancakes for many years.

THINK ABOUT THE MATH

- The phrase "x times as many" can be rewritten as a multiplication equation.
- There are 1,000 mg (milligrams) in 1 g (gram).
- There are 1,000 mL (milliliters) in 1 L (liter).
- Write a multiplication equation to compare sizes of things.
- Use smaller units to express and define larger measurement units.
- Use diagrams that show a measurement scale to show measurement quantities.

*Adapted from *The Marvelous Exploits of Paul Bunyan* by W.B. Laughead

NAME _____ DATE _____

Directions: Use page 73 to answer these questions. First, skim the paragraphs to find information that might help you solve the problem. Remember to show your thinking as you do the math!

1 How much does the storyteller claim mosquitoes weigh today? _____

An actual mosquito weighs 2.5 mg.

What is the difference in the mosquito weight mentioned in the story and actual mosquitoes today? Express your answer in both milligrams and grams.

2 What does the storyteller claim is the length of mosquitoes today? _____

The actual size of a mosquito is .5 cm to 2 cm.

Draw a number-line diagram to compare the mosquito sizes mentioned in the story and their actual size.

3 How many bumblebees did Sourdough Sam bring out? _____

Based on the description of the mosquitoes, what do you imagine was the size of the bees? _____

4 How much liquid sugar (nectar) could the bees' stomachs hold? _____

The honey stomach of an actual bumblebee holds less than 1 mL.

Based on this information, how many times larger were the bees' stomachs in the story than those of actual bumblebees?

NAME _____ DATE _____

Directions: Look back at the passage and think about the unique characteristics of tall tales. If possible, research to learn more about tall tales before you write your own.

1 Why do you think tall tales use exaggeration? What purpose does this technique serve?

_____

_____

_____

2 In the Paul Bunyan story, why was the solution worse than the original problem?

_____

_____

3 Think of one of your favorite stories. Write notes about the story in the first column. In the second column, write ways you could exaggerate the story details.

	As Written	**Tall Tale**
Character		
Character		
Setting—place		
Setting—time		
Story event		
Story event		
Story event		
Conflict		
Conclusion / Ending		

4 On a separate sheet of paper, rewrite the story as a tall tale, referring to your chart in question 3. Illustrate your story and share it with classmates.

NAME _____   DATE _____

Race to the Finish

During the summer months, many bicycle races take place around the country. Some races have more than one event. A mid-summer race in central Oregon has five stages. Cyclists compete on courses of different lengths and terrain.

One stage consists of a short race—called a *criterium*—in a downtown area. Streets are blocked off all day for a series of races. Amateur races include various age categories, including some races for kids. The youngest riders race one lap or less. Kids age 8 to 10 race three laps. Each lap might be 1 kilometer (km) long.

The final downtown races are for professional cyclists. They ride the same 1 km course, which has four 90-degree turns. Even though the course is short, pro racers reach high speeds. Teams battle for sprint points and prizes at various stages of the race. A team may have one rider attack or take the lead, forcing other teams to chase. As many as 15,000 spectators line the streets to watch as the cyclists whiz by at speeds of over 50 kilometers per hour (kph)! The crowd cheers for their favorite team and rings bells or clappers on the laps that qualify for prizes.

NAME _____ DATE _____

| **Problem Solving** | **Directions:** Use page 76 to answer these questions. First, skim the paragraphs to find information that might help you solve the problem. Remember to show your thinking as you do the math! |

1 The average speed for riders in a race was 50 kph. If the race lasted 60 minutes, about how many laps did most riders complete? _____

About how many kilometers did they ride? _____

2 A final race lasted 75 minutes. How long did the race last in hours? _____

The first cyclist completed 50 laps. How long did it take him to ride one lap? _____

Explain how you found the answer to this question.

3 Draw a picture of the downtown race course. What shape is the course?

_____

4 One race has a final stage with a circuit course. Men race 5 laps, or 83 kilometers. How long is each lap? Show the remainder as a fraction.

_____

Draw a number line to illustrate the length of the laps the cyclists rode.

The women race 3 laps for a total course length of 51 kilometers. How long is one lap?

_____

NAME _____   DATE _____

Engage   **Directions:** Refer to the passage and questions on pages 76–77 to practice working with time and distance while solving these additional problems.

1 If a cyclist in the women's circuit course rides 34 kph, how long will it take her to complete the course?

Use this formula: Time = Distance ÷ Speed.

_____

2 The criterium course is 5 blocks long and 1 block wide. Each block is about 100 meters long and 100 meters wide. What is the perimeter of the race course?

3 In the kids' race, one rider averaged 9 km per hour. How long would it take that cyclist to ride 3 laps?

Use equations and visual models to solve the problem and explain your thinking.

_____

4 Think about how far it is to walk or ride a bike to get to school or a friend's house. How many blocks is it? Draw a simple map of your route.

Is the number of blocks less than or greater than the number of blocks in question 2 above? _____

About how many minutes do you think it takes to walk or ride this distance?

_____

How many minutes do you think it would take you to ride around the criterium course in question 2? _____

Write an equation to show how long it would take you to complete a race of 3 laps around the criterium course.

NAME _____   DATE _____

Traveling to School

"How many of you have measured the distance you live from school?" Mrs. Gavin looked around the room.

Connor shrugged. He didn't know exactly how far he lived from the school, but he walked to school, as did many of his friends.

The teacher sketched the school, the post office, and other landmarks. "Most of you probably live about half a mile from school, as far away as the post office, or maybe a little farther. We also have some families who live in a subdivision on the other side of the mall, a little over two miles away. And there are students who live all the distances in between."

Kids around the room shrugged. Connor thought Mrs. Gavin's talk would be more interesting if it were about something other than school.

She continued. "You've probably noticed the pedestrian walkway over the freeway and new sidewalks in the neighborhood. The school district hopes that with these safety measures, more of you will be able to walk to school."

Connor doodled a shining sun on the corner of his notebook page. If the weather was good, walking was fine. In the winter, well . . .

"This would reduce the number of students who will ride a bus, and the district could use the money for other things, like technology."

At Mrs. Gavin's last statement, the class roused a bit. More technology sounded like new computer equipment. Connor sat up, interested to see what was coming next.

THINK ABOUT THE MATH

- On a line plot, each data value is shown as an X or a dot above a number line.

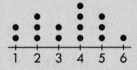

- Data may be measured in fractions of a unit.
- Compare fractions to a benchmark fraction, such as $\frac{1}{2}$.
- Fractions and mixed numbers can be placed between whole numbers on a number line.
- Use a number line to compare fractions.

Distance from School	Total Number of Students	Walk	Car	School Bus
less than $\frac{1}{4}$ mile	76	$\frac{3}{4}$ of students	$\frac{1}{4}$ of students	
$\frac{1}{4}$–$\frac{1}{2}$ mile	24	$\frac{1}{2}$ of students	$\frac{1}{2}$ of students	
$\frac{1}{2}$–1 mile	100	$\frac{1}{2}$ of students	$\frac{1}{4}$ of students	$\frac{1}{4}$ of students
1–2 miles	76	$\frac{1}{4}$ of students	$\frac{1}{4}$ of students	$\frac{1}{2}$ of students
over 2 miles	198		$\frac{1}{3}$ of students	$\frac{2}{3}$ of students

NAME _____   DATE _____

Directions: Use the passage and chart on page 79 and work with classmates to answer the questions below.

1 Use the information from the chart on the previous page to complete the chart below.

Use multiplication, division, or fraction models to find the fractional number of each total. Use the back of this page or another sheet of paper to do the math.

What is the number of students in each distance range that take each form of transportation to school?

Distance from School	Total Number of Students	Walk	Car	School Bus
less than $\frac{1}{4}$ mile	76			
$\frac{1}{4}$–$\frac{1}{2}$ mile	24			
$\frac{1}{2}$–1 mile	100			
1–2 miles	76			
over 2 miles	198			

2 Which category has the greatest number of students? _____

3 Which categories have no students? _____

_____

4 How many students attend Connor's school in all? _____

5 Which fraction is greater, $\frac{1}{3}$ or $\frac{2}{3}$? Explain how you know using "$\frac{1}{2}$" in your answer.

_____

_____

_____

6 How might this information help the people who plan school bus routes for Connor's school?

_____

_____

NAME _____ DATE _____

Engage

Directions: Write one or more questions that represent a problem or issue for your class or school. Work with classmates to generate data about students in your class that would provide information to help solve the problem. Use the data to practice constructing a line plot. On a separate sheet of paper, write and answer questions about the data in the line plot that suggest possible solutions to the problem.

_____

_____

_____

_____

_____

NAME _____   DATE _____

Sand Dunes

Sand dunes form in places that have an abundance of loose sand with no plants. A prevailing wind moves the sand across the earth. Dunes form when there is a place for the sand to pile up. Sand can be obstructed by shrubs, rocks, or mountains. Any obstacle in the topography can cause sand to pile up. As the amount of sand increases, ripples and dunes form. Sometimes dunes stack on top of other dunes that were formed earlier.

The shape and size of sand dunes is affected by various factors. The direction and velocity of the wind makes a difference. Another factor is the type of sand that makes up the dune. The wind moves the sand along the inclined slope. It reaches the crest and slips down the other side. In this way, a dune can advance several feet a year. If the direction of the prevailing winds is consistent over a period of time, a dune may shift in that direction. Plants make a dune more stable and make it harder for the sand to shift.

Sand dunes can be over a mile wide and hundreds of feet high. They have different shapes. When a sand dune gets steep enough, the weight makes it collapse. It forms a slope. Each dune's slope has a different angle, depending on the type of sand. The slipface of most sand dunes has an angle of 30 to 34 degrees.

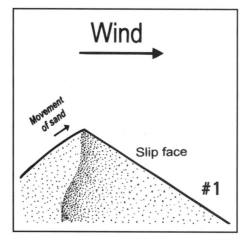

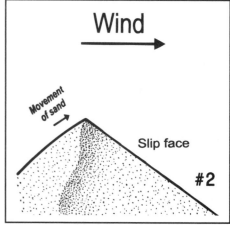

NAME _____ DATE _____

Problem Solving

1 Use a red pencil or crayon to trace the rays that form the angle of sand dune #1 where it meets the ground.

Circle the end point of the angle in blue.

2 How would you describe each ray? _____

_____

3 How would you describe the endpoint of the angle in an actual sand dune?

_____

_____

4 Measure the angle of each sand dune. Write a number sentence to compare the slopes of the two sand dunes.

How would you describe the comparison in words? _____

_____

_____

On which slope do you think wind would have a greater effect? _____

_____

5 Use a protractor to draw a sand dune with a slope of 32 degrees.

NAME _____   **DATE** _____

Engage | **Directions:** Create a model of a sand dune using garden sand or salt. Construct your model in a box or other container.

1 Use a standard unit, such as cups, or use a scale to measure the amount of sand in your sand dune.

Draw a picture of your model.

2 Place a piece of paper on your sand dune to form an angle with the bottom of the container. Work with a classmate to estimate and measure the slope.

Label your drawing in question 1 with the angle measurement.

3 Use an electric or paper fan to create wind.

How does wind direction and speed affect the slope? _____

_____

Use words and pictures to show what happens.

NAME _____ DATE _____

Small Town U.S.A.: North Pole, Alaska

People first observed eclipses long ago. They discovered from the shadow cast during a lunar eclipse that Earth is round. We divide the planet into two hemispheres, or halves of a sphere. The equator is an imaginary line around the center of Earth. It divides the two hemispheres. Place locations are between 0 and 90 degrees north or south of the equator. The equator is 0 degrees latitude and the North Pole is 90 degrees north latitude. The South Pole is 90 degrees south latitude. One degree of latitude equals about 69 miles.

North Pole, Alaska, is a small town not far from Fairbanks. It has a population of just over 2,000. The town is at 64 degrees N latitude. Many people think towns in Alaska receive a lot of snow. The part of Alaska where North Pole is located is drier.

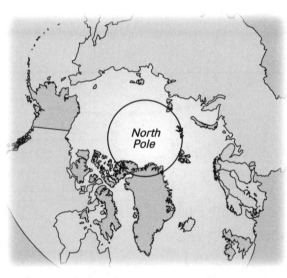

The average rainfall is only 10 inches, and they receive about 62 inches of snow per year. Anchorage and Nome both get over 10 inches more snow per year than North Pole.

The Arctic Circle is an imaginary line around Earth at 66 degrees N latitude. Above this line, the sun does not set on the longest day of the year. It does not rise on the shortest day of the year. The town of North Pole has 21 hours of daylight on the longest day of the year. It is light only about 3 hours on the shortest day of the year! On a cold winter day, there's not much daylight to warm the air. Record temperatures in the winter have hit as low as −65°F.

North Pole, Alaska, is not exactly at the North Pole. It is also not the northernmost town in Alaska, but it is still a unique place to live.

NAME _____ DATE _____

Problem Solving | **Directions:** Use page 85 to answer these questions. First, skim the paragraphs to find information that might help you solve the problem. Remember to show your thinking as you do the math!

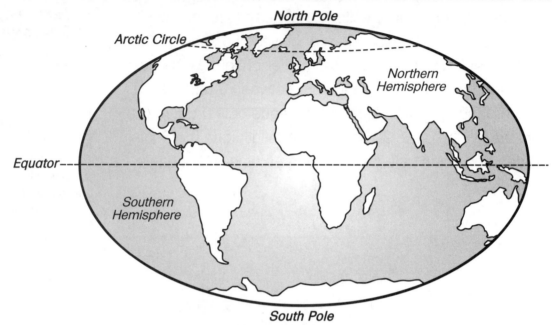

1 About how many miles is North Pole, Alaska from the Arctic Circle?

2 About how many miles is North Pole, Alaska from the geographic North Pole?

3 Look at a map or another resource to find the latitude for your town. How many degrees south of the North Pole do you live? _____

About how many miles is it from your town to the North Pole?

4 How far is your town from the Arctic Circle?

5 How many feet of snow does the town of North Pole receive in an average year? _____

Does your town receive more or less snow than North Pole? _____

Does your town receive more or less rainfall than North Pole? _____

6 On the back of this page, write what you think it would be like to live in North Pole, Alaska. Include details to support your arguments.

NAME _____   DATE _____

Engage

Directions: Use maps and your research on the North Pole ("Matthew Henson: A Frozen Frontier," page 13) to compare information. Use what you have learned to create math problems for classmates to solve.

Think about the questions below and take notes to help you brainstorm ideas for math problems.

1 Compare North Pole, Alaska, with the geographic North Pole. How are they similar? How are they different?

_____

_____

_____

_____

_____

2 What did you learn about the climate of the two places? Think in terms of numbers, such as temperatures.

_____

_____

_____

_____

_____

3 How is the location of each place described geographically?

_____

_____

_____

_____

_____

NAME _____ DATE _____

Optical Illusions

Sometimes we think we see something that is not really there. Or it doesn't appear exactly as it is. What we see doesn't match reality. We call these optical illusions. In some cases, our brain expects to see something. It then processes the visual signals received from the eyes in a way that makes sense with our expectation. As we look at the image or figure longer, it begins to make less sense.

Optical illusions use patterns with lines and shapes that might be misleading. Our brain interprets what we see but it might not match the actual reality.

Different people may see the same image in different ways. We interpret what we see based on our experiences. One well-known example of this type of illusion is a line drawing of a woman. Some people see a picture of a young woman wearing a hat with a feather. Other people view the same picture as that of an older woman with a head scarf.

Optical illusions are fun puzzles to think about. Learning to see things in different ways helps us with problem solving. It can also help us think of new and creative ideas.

Image courtesy of the Library of Congress, Prints & Photographs Division, LC-DIG-ds-00175.

#8389 Real-World Math Problem Solving   88   *©Teacher Created Resources*

NAME _____   DATE _____

Problem Solving **Directions:** Refer to the passage on page 88 and use what you know about lines and shapes to answer the questions.

1 Draw a 5 cm line segment. At each end of the line segment, draw an arrow pointing toward the line.

Directly under the first line segment, draw another 5 cm line segment. At each end of the line segment, draw an arrow pointing away from the line.

Which line segment appears to be longer? _____

Why do you think this is? _____

2 The context of lines affects the way we see those lines. Are the heavy black lines in the figure below straight or curved? What affects your thoughts about the lines? How can you prove your answer?

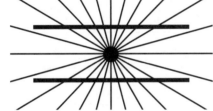

_____

_____

_____

3 What shapes are in the figure below? If we assume this figure is an open book, is it open toward you or away from you? Discuss with a classmate how each of you sees the picture. Why might your answers be the same or different?

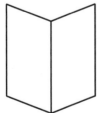

_____

_____

_____

4 How shapes are put together affects the way we see and interpret each shape. Is the top of the first shape the same width as the top of the second shape? How can you prove your answer?

#1 _____

#2 _____

NAME _____ DATE _____

1 Draw points, line segments, rays, and angles in different patterns and figures. How can you make your classmates think they see something different than what is actually there?

2 Try drawing parallel or perpendicular lines in different combinations. Can you draw parallel lines that don't appear parallel? Can you draw perpendicular lines that don't look perpendicular?

3 How can you combine different shapes to create an optical illusion? What difference does it make if shapes are congruent? Experiment by drawing various shapes on the back of this page.

_____

_____

_____

4 Write a few sentences to describe your experiences with the optical illusions on page 89. What helped you or kept you from realizing how each illusion worked? Discuss your answers with classmates.

_____

_____

_____

5 Write a few sentences to describe your experiences trying to create your own optical illusions. What do you think made the task easy or difficult? Discuss your answers with classmates.

_____

_____

_____

NAME _____   DATE _____

Sundials

"How does a clock work?" Mr. Hanson read from the slip of paper he had pulled from the question box. "Good question, Kayla. We'll find out today as we continue to learn about shadows."

Mr. Hanson displayed pictures on the whiteboard for everyone to see. The pictures showed flat, round stones with numerals carved into them and a piece of metal pointing up at an angle. "These are sundials," he explained. "People have used sundials for hundreds of years to keep track of time. As Earth rotates, the sun moves across the sky, creating shadows."

Kayla nodded and raised her hand. "But when we measured our shadows, we were standing straight up, not leaning over like the objects in those pictures."

The teacher pointed to the metal part of one of the pictures. "We know that when a shadow from a vertical object is the shortest, it is noon. Objects cast longer shadows in the morning and late afternoon, when the sun is closer to the horizon. But when we try to tell time using our own shadows it won't always be correct. Can anyone explain this?"

Chad practically jumped out of his seat. He always knew the answers to science stuff like this. Kayla watched as Chad used his hands to illustrate as he talked. "Earth spins on its axis, which is tilted at an angle. If we put the vertical part of a sundial at an angle, it makes up for the tilt of Earth."

"Yes." Mr. Hanson displayed another picture of Earth in rotation around the sun. "Since we do have clocks, we can use them to make sure we use the correct angles on our sundials."

> ### THINK ABOUT THE MATH
>
> - Roman numerals are a different numbering system than our Arabic numerals.
> - A ray is a part of a line that extends in one direction from a single point.
> - An angle is formed by two rays that have a common endpoint and are not part of the same line.
> - A circle is said to be 360 degrees.
> - Use a protractor to measure angles in degrees.
> - Use a model to determine the type of angle in a figure.

NAME _____   DATE _____

Directions: Use page 91 to answer these questions. First, skim the paragraphs to find information that might help you solve the problem. Remember to show your thinking as you do the math!

1 How would you describe the numerals on the sundial in the photograph on the right?

_____

_____

_____

_____

2 What do the numbers represent? _____

3 What shape is the base of the sundial? _____

How does this relate to what a sundial represents? _____

_____

_____

4 Draw and label a picture of a sundial. What geometric figures did you include in your drawing?

_____

_____

_____

_____

_____

_____

Photograph by Louisa Mac, CC BY 2.0.

NAME _____   DATE _____

> **Engage** | **Directions:** Research with classmates to explore and learn more about sundials and keeping time.

1 Roman numerals are often used on sundials. How does the numbering system work?

_____

_____

_____

2 What differences, if any, do you think there might be in sundials used in the northern hemisphere and the southern hemisphere?

_____

_____

_____

How would you explain any differences? _____

_____

_____

_____

3 What differences, if any, do you think there would be between a sundial used at or near the equator and a sundial used closer to the North or South Pole?

_____

_____

_____

NAME _____   DATE _____

Cozy Quilts

Daniel knocked on the door and waited for his aunt to answer. Mia's long snout and pointed ears greeted him at the door. He enjoyed visiting his aunt and uncle, petting the German shepherds, seeing how things were growing in his uncle's garden, and looking at his aunt's latest quilt.

"What's happening today?" Daniel asked around Mia's enthusiastic welcome.

"Your uncle is picking tomatoes, and I'm working on a new quilt. Which do you want to see first?" Daniel's aunt gave him a one-armed hug across his shoulders.

"Your quilt. Sometimes the tomato plants have worms and they're gross." He made a face. "I'll sample the tomatoes once he gets them picked, though. Nothing better than a fresh tomato from the garden!"

Daniel followed his aunt into her sewing room. He liked all the different designs that could be made. He enjoyed experimenting with the colors, shapes, and patterns. Then the best part was that he didn't have just a drawing or toy when he was finished. The end result would be a quilt that would keep someone warm in the winter while reading books or playing games.

His aunt showed him her current project, then sat at her sewing machine to work on it. Daniel wandered around until he found fabric, in colors he liked, already cut into pieces. He picked up some triangles and began to arrange them, adding shapes as he went along.

NAME _____ DATE _____

Problem Solving | **Directions:** Use page 94 to answer these questions. First, skim the paragraphs to find information that might help you solve the problem. Remember to show your thinking as you do the math!

1 What shapes are in the quilt? Notice parallel or perpendicular lines, number and types of angles, etc., to identify the shapes.

_____

_____

_____

_____

2 Name and define specific shapes in the quilt.

_____

_____

_____

3 Draw and label the specific shapes to show how you know what they are.

4 Each part of the design forms a "quilt block." Which block(s) have a line of symmetry? (Color is not a factor.)

_____

_____

5 What designs could Daniel have made with the shapes he found? What other shapes could he add to the design?

_____

_____

NAME _____   DATE _____

Engage   **Directions:** Create a model for a quilt design. Then, answer the questions below.

1 Use a ruler, pattern blocks, or other templates to create and draw a design for a quilt block. Color your design.

2 Which shapes did you include in your design? Why?

_____

_____

_____

_____

_____

_____

_____

3 Does your design have a line of symmetry? How does your decision whether or not to have symmetry affect the overall design?

_____

_____

_____

4 Compare your drawing to a classmate's. How are the designs similar? How are they different?

_____

_____

_____

NAME _____   DATE _____

Gulliver's Travels*

They led me into the palace and into the king's chamber. He was seated on his throne, with his best aides in attendance. In front of the throne I saw a large table filled with globes and spheres and all kinds of mathematical instruments. His majesty paid no attention to us, even though there were enough of us that we made some noise. He was deep in a mathematical problem, and we waited at least an hour before he could solve it.

As soon as one of his aides noticed he had stopped thinking about the problem, one of them gently struck his mouth. The other struck his right ear. These were signs that he should listen and speak to his audience. He looked at us and remembered he had been told of our visit. Another aide came up to give me a flap on my ear, but I made signs to tell him I didn't need the reminder, as I was able to pay attention.

The king asked me several questions. I answered in every language I knew, but I could not understand him, and he could not understand me. He ordered me to an apartment in his palace. A prince, who was known for his hospitality to strangers, escorted me. Two additional servants were appointed to attend to me.

Four men who had been with the king did me the honor of dining with me. We had two courses, of three dishes each. In the first course, a shoulder of mutton was cut into an equilateral triangle. A piece of beef was cut into a rhombus shape. The pudding was a circle. The second course had ducks shaped like fiddles and sausages like flutes. A breast of veal was shaped as a harp. The servants cut our bread into cones, cylinders, and parallelograms. Other foods were cut into other mathematical shapes.

During dinner, I boldly asked the names of things in their language. They delighted to give me answers, sure that once I could talk with them, I would see and admire their great mathematical abilities.

> ### THINK ABOUT THE MATH
>
> - A quadrilateral has four angles.
> - A parallelogram is a quadrilateral that has opposite sides that are equal in length and parallel.
> - A rhombus is an equilateral parallelogram, with all sides equal, that may or may not have oblique angles.
> - Identify the number and type of angles to name and classify two-dimensional figures.
> - Determine if a two-dimensional figure has parallel and/or perpendicular lines to name and classify the figure.

*Excerpt from *Gulliver's Travels* by Jonathan Swift

NAME _____   DATE _____

Problem Solving **Directions:** Use page 97 to answer these questions. First, skim the paragraphs to find information that might help you solve the problem. Remember to show your thinking as you do the math!

1 What shape was the shoulder of mutton?

_____

Draw the shape and list its attributes. Label the measurements of your drawing.

2 What shape was the piece of beef in the first course?

_____

Draw the shape and list its attributes. Label the measurements of your drawing.

3 Describe the pudding. Draw a picture to illustrate your explanation.

_____

4 List the shapes of the bread and their attributes. _____

_____

_____

Draw pictures to illustrate your definitions.

NAME _____ **DATE** _____

1 Gulliver mentions that "other foods were cut into other mathematical shapes." What other foods do you suppose might have been served?

_____

_____

2 What shapes might describe those foods? _____

_____

_____

Draw and label pictures of the foods.

3 Think of the foods that are in your favorite meal. Draw and label pictures of the foods.

4 Make a list of the shapes of the foods in your favorite meal. Next to the name of each shape, list its attributes.

_____

_____

_____

_____

NAME _____   DATE _____

Urban Symmetry

Adrian glanced at his homework page. He didn't like homework because it took time away from basketball. But this assignment intrigued him. He was supposed to look at different buildings and identify shapes. He might have thought that was too easy, except the teacher asked them also to look for lines of symmetry and how that might affect the structure's design or function.

He dropped his backpack on the table and grabbed an apple from the fruit bowl. Adrian picked up the cordless phone and showed it to Grandma. "I'm going to call Nick so we can do our homework together, okay?"

"Will he come here?" Grandma looked up from the magazine she was reading.

"Yes, but then we have to take a walk in the neighborhood and take notes. We'll stay together as buddies, don't worry." Adrian stood by her chair and munched on his apple.

Grandma patted his hand. "Don't be gone too long, and be careful!"

Adrian talked to Nick and then waited for him to arrive. While he waited, he mapped a route they could walk that would take them by interesting buildings and would take them less than an hour to walk.

"Hey, I mapped out a route for us." Adrian handed the paper to Nick as soon as he came in. "We'll see interesting buildings and other things, and it will take us less than an hour."

"Great!" Nick took a notebook and a pencil from his backpack and followed Adrian out the door.

NAME _____   DATE _____

Directions: Use page 100 and the photographs below to answer these questions. Remember to show your thinking as you do the math!

1 Why does the building in the photo on the right have an unusual shape?

_____

_____

_____

2 How would you describe the streets on the photo to the right?

_____

_____

_____

3 Draw the line of symmetry on the photo to the right. Does it make a difference to the structure's function or design? Why or why not?

_____

_____

_____

_____

4 Trace any shapes you see in the structure in the photo on the right. What angles or types of lines help you define the shape(s)?

_____

_____

_____

_____

NAME _____ DATE _____

Engage | **Directions:** Work together with a classmate. Discuss shapes and angles in architecture to answer the questions below.

---

1 Look around the room. Draw a structure you see. Use a colored pencil to trace any angles. List the type(s) of angles in your drawing.

2 What shape(s) make up the structure? Write the name of each shape and its characteristics.

_____

_____

_____

_____

3 Does the structure you observed have a line of symmetry? Why might this be important?

_____

_____

4 How do the features (angles, shapes) of the structure affect how it works?

_____

_____

5 On a separate sheet of paper, design an office building, school, or other structure for your community. What angles and shapes would it need to have to be well suited for its purpose? Use what you know about shapes and angles to explain your answer.

_____

_____

_____

_____

Answer Key

Wolves & Coyotes (pages 7–9)

Problem Solving: 1. $24 \times a = 60$; $20 \times 3 = 60$; A small wolf weighs about 3 times as much as a small coyote; $45 \times b = 120$; $50 \times 2 = 100$; A large wolf weighs about 2 times as much as a large coyote. **2.** wolf: 5 ft. × 12 in. per foot = 60 in.; 6 ft. × 12 in. per foot = 72 in.; 60–72 in.; coyote: 3 ft. × 12 in. per foot = 36 in. + $\frac{1}{2}$ of 12 in. per foot = 6 in.; 36 + 6 = 42 in.; 4 ft. × 12 in. per foot = 48 in. + $\frac{1}{2}$ of 12 in. per foot = 6 in.; 48 + 6 = 54 in.; 42–54 in. **3.** wolf: 2 feet 3 in. to 2 feet 9 in. or 2–3 feet; coyote: 1 ft. 8 in. to 1 ft. 10 in.; a little less than 2 feet **4.** 100 sq. miles in United States × c = 300 sq. miles in Canada = 3 times larger north of the United States **5.** $\frac{1}{5}$; $\frac{1}{5}$ × (of) 60 sq. miles = 60 ÷ 5 = 12; 12 sq. miles

Engage: 1. Answers will vary but may include differences in size, physical characteristics, and behavior. **2.** Answers will vary but may include how coyotes can live in urban areas with abundant prey and thus need a smaller territory; wolves in areas where prey may be scarce at some times of the year require a larger territory. **3.** Answers will vary. **4.** Answers will vary but may include that the wolf is more endangered than the coyote. **5.** Answers will vary.

My Shadow (pages 10–12)

Problem Solving: 1. $127 = 33x$, $x = 3$ R28, so about 4 times longer in the morning than at noon; $62 = 33x$, $x = 1$ R29, so about 2 times longer in the late afternoon; $201 - 127 = 74$ inches **2.** 64 inches tall; in the late afternoon **3.** Answers will vary.

Engage: 1. When an object obstructs light from a light source, a shadow is formed; a screen behind the object will turn dark where the light is obstructed. **2.** Our bodies cast the shadow on the ground; our feet touch the ground, so the shadow remains connected to our feet. **3.** the changes in the sun's position in the sky **4.** It was before the sun was up to cast a shadow. **5.** They can help us determine the time of day.

Matthew Henson: A Frozen Frontier (pages 13–15)

Problem Solving: 1. $170 ÷ 5 = 34$ miles per day; $170 ÷ 4$ = over 42 miles per day **2.** $12 \times b = 34$; $12 \times 2 = 24$ and $12 \times 3 = 36$; 36 is closer to 34, so about 3 miles per hour; 14×3 = about 42 miles per day **3.** $90 - 87 = 3$ degrees **4.** 3 hours × 2 miles per hour = 6 miles; They go 5 miles, so they travel less than 2 miles per hour.

Engage: 1. It is the northernmost point on Earth. **2.** Polaris, the "north star," which almost never changes position, is aligned with the North Pole. **3.** The sun is almost always above the horizon (no sunrise or sunset) in the summer and almost always below the horizon (no sunrise or sunset) in the winter. There is one sunrise per year in March and one sunset per year in September. **4.** none; It is in the middle of the Arctic Ocean. **5.** The North Pole because it is at lower elevation (sea level) than the South Pole. **6.** Answers will vary.

Jack S. Kilby: Inventor of the Microchip (pages 16–18)

Problem Solving: 1. $6\frac{3}{10}$ cubic inches; Number line should show inch marks with increments of 10 within 1 inch, marked off as $6\frac{3}{10}$. **2.** less; 10 ounces < 1 pound **3.** 50×10 ounces = 500 ounces; pounds **4.** $587 \times 14 = 8{,}218 \approx 8{,}200$

Engage: 1. Answers will vary but might include hard-working, determined, and creative. **2.** Answers will vary but might include he thought it was important to work hard for an education. **3.** Answers will vary but might include small size or no wires. **4.** Answers will vary but may include invention of the microchip/integrated circuit and handheld calculator; work with solar power **5.** Nobel Prize in Physics

Grand Canyon Adventure (pages 19–21)

Problem Solving: 1. Answers will vary but might include 2 families of 12, 3 families of 8, 4 families of 6, 6 families of 4, 8 families of 3, 12 families of 2, and other possible combinations, such as 4 families of 5 and 1 family of 4, etc. **2.** 11 is a prime number; Its only factors are 1 and 11. **3.** Answers will vary but might include 4 quarters (4 × 25¢), 10 dimes (10 × 10¢), 2 half dollars (2 × 50¢), 1 half dollar and 2 quarters (50¢ + 2 × 25¢), 20 nickels (20 × 5¢) or various other combinations. **4.** 20 pictures; 120 pictures on 1 day, 60 pictures on 2 days, 40 pictures on 3 days, 30 pictures on 4 days, 24 pictures on 5 days, 20 pictures on 6 days

Engage: 1. no; 23 miles does not divide evenly into 2 parts; They could go 11 miles during one part and 12 miles during the other part. **2.** $18 × 5 = $90 **3.** 6 days; $30 ÷ 6 days = $5 per day **4.** $76 × 2 = $152; $86 × 2 = $172; $6 × 4 = $24; 152 + 172 + 24 = $348; $92 **5.** 7,000 − 2,400 = 4,600 foot drop in elevation

A Walk Through the Neighborhood (pages 22–24)

Problem Solving: 1. Add 8. **2.** Even numbers are on the north side of the street and odd numbers are on the south side of the street; south side **3.** west **4.** a cross-street intersection **5.** Answers will vary but may include only a few houses fit on each block, other cross streets, vacant lots, etc.

Engage: 1. 60 feet road-front footage ÷ 15 feet per number = 4 number increments between houses **2.** 300 foot block ÷ 60 feet road-front footage per city lot = 5 houses **3.–4.** Answers will vary.

Freeway Art (pages 25–27)

Problem Solving: 1. circles, rectangles **2.** After a solid block, there are three consecutive blocks broken up by horizontal and vertical line segments. **3.** lines, arches; the top images repeat; Answers will vary.

Engage: 1. Drawing should be shaped like a trapezoid; Answers will vary but may include earth or dirt absorbing the noise. **2.** planting trees or other plants; gravel or rocks **3.** Answers will vary but may include horizontal and vertical patterns, shapes used in a pattern or at random; interesting but not distracting; Answers will vary. **4.–5.** Answers will vary.

The Transcontinental Railroad (pages 28–30)

Problem Solving: 1. $\frac{200}{5,000}$ (divide numerator and denominator by 2) $= \frac{100}{2,500}$ (divide numerator and denominator by 100) $= \frac{1}{25}$ **2.** $\frac{14,000}{50,000}$ (divide numerator and denominator by factor of 2) $= \frac{7,000}{25,000}$ (divide numerator and denominator by 1,000) $= \frac{7}{25}$ **3.** 1,659 days; 365; $365 \times y = 1,659$; $400 \times y = 1,600$; about 4 years (actually 4 years, 199 days)

Engage: 1. $40 \times 6,400$ acres of land = 256,000 acres of land ($4 \times 6,400 = 25,600$; multiply this by 10 = 256,000) **2.** $350 \times 25 = 8,750$ iron rails; $2,500 \times 25 = 62,500$ wooden ties; $10,000 \times 25 = 250,000$ spikes **3.** 40 miles × $16,000 = $640,000

Amaranth: An Edible Weed (pages 31–33)

Problem Solving: 1. eight thousand years **2.** 100 years in a century; $6,000 \div 100 = 60$ centuries ago to $8,000 \div 100 = 80$ centuries ago **3.** 1,000,000 (one million) **4.** 939 acres; about 94 acres **5.** 12 inches × 6 feet = 72 inches; 72 inches ÷ 3 inches per day = 24 days **6.** $939 < 200,000$

Engage: 1. Answers will vary but may include pigs like to eat it and it grows like a weed. **2.** Answers will vary but may include nutrient value and the fact that it is easy to grow and is a gluten-free grain-type food. **3.** Answers will vary but may include it can take over other crops farmers try to grow, it reproduces quickly, adapts and grows easily, and is resistant to weed control measures. **4.–5.** Answers will vary.

The Mighty Mississippi (pages 34–36)

Problem Solving: 1. $1 \times a = 3$; 3 times as fast **2.** $5,280 \times 2$ miles = 10,560 feet; $10,560 - 30 = 10,530$ feet wider **3.** $3 \times b = 200$; $66\frac{2}{3}$ times deeper; about 70 times deeper **4.** 1,500 foot drop in elevation; 1,475 feet > 1,454 feet; The distance the river drops in elevation is more than the height of the building; if the river were a waterfall all in one place, the waterfall would be higher than the Empire State building.

Engage: 1. Mighty Mississippi, Ol' Man River, The Big Muddy; Answers will vary but might include the size of the river and amount of sediment carried. **2.** commercial shipping; recreational **3.** to aid in shipping, not for flood control; make it wider and deeper **4.** Answers will vary but may include navigation and environmental reasons, such as water and land management (flood control). **5.–6.** Answers will vary.

The Gettysburg Address (pages 37–39)

Problem Solving: 1. four score = $20 \times 4 = 80$ years + 7 years = 87 years before 1863; $1863 - 87 = 1776$; the signing of the Declaration of Independence **2.** [current year] $- 1863 = a$ **3.** $94,000 - 72,000 = 22,000$ more soldiers **4.** $\frac{1}{2}$ of 12,500 = 6,250; ($\frac{1}{2}$ of 12,000 = 6,000; $\frac{1}{2}$ of 500 = 250); Pickett sent 12,500 out of 72,000 men total; round 12,500 to 13,000; divide both by 1,000 to reduce to $\frac{13}{72}$; long division results in answer of .18 (rounded to nearest hundredth), which is less than one quarter of his total army or over one tenth of the army **5.** $46,000 - 8,000 = 38,000$

Engage: 1. Answers will vary but may include that it will endure and stand through the Civil War. **2.** that the nation was founded on a principle that all men are created equal **3.** Answers will vary; to dedicate a field where soldiers were buried; the dedication of the Soldier's National Cemetery in Gettysburg, Pennsylvania **4.** Answers will vary but may include that they sacrificed their lives for their country, for freedom, etc. **5.** Answers will vary but might include devoting themselves to and advancing the cause for freedom for all and the ideals of the government by the people.

The Eagle (pages 40–42)

Problem Solving: 1. 150 ÷ 60 minutes in an hour = 15 ÷ 6 = $2\frac{1}{2}$ miles per minute **2.** 120 ÷ 60 minutes in an hour = 12 ÷ 6 = 2 miles per minute **3.** 760 ÷ 10 = 76 and 60 ÷ 10 = 6, so 76 ÷ 6 = 12 R4, about 13 miles per minute **4.** 150 miles per hour > 120 miles per hour; 150 miles per hour < 760 miles per hour **5.** *Suggested answer.*

Peregrine Falcon	200 mph	$3\frac{1}{3}$ miles per minute
Golden Eagle	150 mph	$2\frac{1}{2}$ miles per minute
Red-tailed Hawk	120 mph	2 miles per minute
Barn owl	50 mph	$\frac{5}{6}$ mile per minute

Engage: 1. About half of them start with the same consonant sound, /k/; Answers will vary. **2.** hyperbole: The eagle is not really close to the sun; personification: The lands are not actually lonely. **3.** Answers will vary but may include *crag, azure, wrinkled, thunderbolt*. **4.–5.** Answers will vary.

Montana Sapphires (pages 43–45)

Problem Solving: 1. 1,000 g; 1,000,000 mg; 5,000 carats; $\frac{1}{5}$ **2.** 12 carats × 200 mg = 2,400 mg; 2.4 g **3.** less than 1 cm **4.** 6,100 cm **5.** $1.2 \times t = 2.4$; since $12 \times 2 = 24$, $1.2 \times 2 = 2.4$; 2 times wider

Engage: 1. [current date] $-$ 150 years **2.** igneous **3.** Sapphires are very hard (second only to diamond). **4.** man-made; Natural sapphires might have more value in the market when sold as gemstones. **5.** hexagon **6.** Answers will vary.